Hard by
the Cloud House

Peter Walker

Hard by
the Cloud House

M

MASSEY UNIVERSITY PRESS

For J. T.
And in memory of J. V.

Te Hokioi on high! Te Hokioi on high!
Sleeping companion of the thunder god,
Where she dwells high above, and
hard by the Cloud House
— *Māori lore*

You quell the thunder and forked
lightning, golden lyre . . . and the eagle
sleeps on the sceptre of the god
— *Pindar*

I've been circling for a thousand years
and I still don't know — am I a falcon,
a storm or a great song?
— *Rainer Maria Rilke*

Contents

I

To Honeycomb Hill

Chapter 1

Late one afternoon in March 1860 a man in a thin green velveteen jacket and a wide-awake hat arrived on foot at a sheep station named Glenmark, about 65 kilometres north of Christchurch. The man was in his mid-fifties but he looked older. Several people who met him that day agreed later that he looked 'careworn', although they could not agree whether his corduroy trousers were patched or not. Earlier in the day he was given a glass of ale by the landlord of the Kōwai pub, 25 kilometres south of Glenmark, and then, after watching him closely, the landlord sent out another ale and a free meal.

The man, whose name was Henry Davis, took to the road again. For a few miles he got a ride on a passing wagon. By mid-afternoon the wind began to blow and rain could be seen whitening in the foothills to the south. As Davis walked towards the farm house at Glenmark, about a mile from the road, rain began falling and he encountered the manager and part-owner of the station coming from the stockyards. With a piercing gaze, tall, handsome — when he was 80 he was still 'slim as a youngster and straight as a gun barrel', a neighbour recalled — George Moore was already one of the richest men in the colony. He saw the stranger and stopped.

'What do you want?'

'I'm looking for work.'

For a man to turn up at a remote station asking for work was well within the normal run of things. The population of the new colony of Canterbury was small, the roads few and the nights very dark. By 1860 there was a little army of swagmen walking from place to place looking for work and, if there was no work available, for shelter and food. It was regarded as a plain duty to provide these. Obituaries for wealthy men often included the sentence 'No swagman was ever turned away'.

'What do you do?' asked Moore.

'I'm a hurdle-maker.'

'There's no such work here.'

Davis then asked if he could stay the night in the men's hut.

Moore: 'I don't run a hotel. There's public accommodation at Weka Pass. Six miles if you go back and take the road. Three miles if you go over the hills.'

They regarded each other for a few moments, the rich man and the poor man, then turned away, never to meet again.

The rain was now coming down in earnest and darkness fell early because of it. Davis must have seen a light at a window because he then knocked at the door of a hut where a carpenter named John Henry lived with his wife. Henry also refused Davis shelter.

A week later he told a Christchurch court what happened: 'He asked for a drink of water which I gave him, as I had no tea at the time. He said "I have just seen Mr. Moore who has denied me stopping here this dreadful wet night: what shall I do?"

'[He] attempted to come into the hut, but I refused, and said that Mr Moore had on a former occasion accused me of having had two men at the place . . . I directed him to the woolshed about three or four hundred yards distant, where he would find shelter. It was raining heavily all night while I was awake. About midnight I heard the dogs barking, and I said to my wife that poor man has lost his way, I think.'[1]

That was a Wednesday night.

Davis was nowhere to be seen the next morning and his existence was therefore forgotten. Glenmark was by then a vast estate, about 60,000 acres, and days or weeks might have passed before he was found but in fact it was only one day later that a shepherd saw a man in the distance, apparently sleeping in the sun: 'On Friday morning last, March 9th, between 8 and 9 o'clock, I saw a man lying on the ground about a mile from the station, near the direction of the Pass.

'He was lying on his back with one leg crossed over the other and his arms spread out, his hat lying about twenty yards from him. I thought he was sleeping, but as I saw no motion as I was calling to my dog, I then thought that he was dead. I went forward and saw some spots of blood on his face and a four-barrelled pistol lying at his feet . . .'

If the barking of the dogs heard by John Henry was a reliable indicator, Davis had killed himself about midnight. He had never found the woolshed. There was no path to follow over the hill to Weka Pass. For four hours, in other words, he had floundered in darkness and rain and travelled a mile.

When news of the incident became known there was public outrage. The new colony was a Church of England settlement and rather high-minded. There was not much bother about equality but everyone, according to high-church and high Tory principles, was bound together in a net of rights and duties. There was a special obligation on the rich to look after the poor. 'Shame — a thousand times shame,' said the *Lyttelton Times*, 'to the individual who sent from his door into the waste a famished footsore man, without a chance of reaching shelter or a prospect of a bit to eat ... What man with a spark of feeling would serve a dog so?'

George Moore defended himself coolly at the inquest: 'He could have found his way if he had been the right sort of man by the way I pointed out to him; it was getting dusk ... There might have been room in the hut for several more; but ... I have been imposed upon too often. I refused him because he was in liquor. I smelt him of it. That was one reason ... He did not appear to be feeble; he looked a strong, able man. I am guided by my opinion as to whether men are impostors or looking for work. I considered this man an impostor. I did not think he was really looking for work, although he asked for it.'

Moore himself was, in his own view, very much the right sort of man. He was a Manxman, hard as nails. He regularly walked the 40 miles to Christchurch and if he was caught out in the rain at night he did not flounder about and wish he were dead but climbed into a flax bush and went to sleep. He did not know that Davis was carrying a pistol and would turn it on himself in a fit of despair, and he therefore cannot be entirely blamed for the suicide, but it must have been his contempt for a 'weakling' that led him to more atrocious decisions.

The body had been found about nine o'clock on Friday morning. The farmhands wanted to move it, at least into the woolshed, but Moore forbade this. It seems that no one was allowed even to approach Davis to cover his face. Moore eventually sent a message to the nearest town, but only by the slowest method, a passing dray.

'I had no horse handy,' he told the inquest.

A policeman arrived at Glenmark on Sunday morning. Davis had been dead more than 80 hours and was still lying where he had fallen. His wide-awake, the broad-brimmed hat of felt or straw worn by most male settlers against the strong antipodean sunlight, was still 20 metres from his body. The autumn sun had been shining on the body for two days. Decomposition had set in.

The constable asked if one of the carpenters could make a box to carry the dead man away. Moore refused. His men, he said, worked on contract: he could not order them to do this. In any case, it was Sunday. How could a carpenter possibly work on the Sabbath? The policeman was offered a box that was lying up at the house.

'I looked at it but it was too narrow,' the constable told the court.

Moore then let him have an old sack from the woolshed to carry away the body.

'Mean, hard-hearted, barbarous, blasphemous man!' cried the *Lyttelton Times*. '[We] express our loathing at religion being made an excuse for want of charity. We cannot say with certainty that Mr Moore's offence is within the letter of the law; perhaps it may be. But this we do know — that after this, no hand of a Christian man should clasp that of Mr Moore till he has done penance for his deep crime against the laws of God and man.'

Moore was not in the least moved by this anathema. He was burnt in effigy in Christchurch. What did he care? When he went to town he carried a tent on his back and slept in Market Square. Glenmark expanded from 60,000 to 150,000 acres. He waged war on all sides — 'What do I care for my neighbours?' — and deliberately kept his sheep diseased with scab, so that other runholders would not take their flocks to market across his land. He became known as 'Scabby' Moore. At one point, it is said, he was ordered to cure his sheep of the disease and instead drove mobs off a cliff to die on the beach below.

Any workman at Glenmark seen with a straight back during daylight hours was fired on the spot for slacking. The men naturally hated their master: 'The air turned blue as soon as he had moved out of hearing,' a neighbour recalled. In the Glenmark stockyards, no races were built for drafting the sheep. 'I do not care to employ a shepherd too lazy to lift a sheep over a rail.'

Twenty years after the swagman died, Moore built the most magnificent mansion yet seen in New Zealand. The house had a peculiar feature: there was only one external door, which was at the front. Moore's dread was that, while his back was turned, the servants might spirit away his valuables or hand a piece of bread to a poor man at the kitchen door.

It is pleasing to report that everything Moore built turned to ashes in his own lifetime. Two years after it was completed, the great house burned to the ground. Molten lead poured like rain over the single door. His daughter

Annie, a spinster, rushed in and out to save her canaries, carrying them to a Wellingtonia tree in the middle of the lawn, but the tree also caught fire and Miss Moore herself was 'much scorched'.

A few years later the vast estate was broken up under threat of government expropriation. Moore then retired to Christchurch, where he went blind. Annie saw her chance and married the family doctor. Moore never knew. He sat in the dark in his mansion on Park Terrace listening out for wayfarers and treasure hunters, unaware that the greatest prize, Annie, had already given herself away.

Long before, he had quarrelled with his wife and his three sons and broken off contact with them and there he died in Park Terrace, sightless, friendless, deceived, and he would have soon been forgotten in the special oblivion which races to erase all memory of those who live selfish lives except for one strange circumstance: a magnificent creature, one of the great productions of evolution — the largest eagle that ever flew — was named after him.

Harpagornis moorei.

At first the reasons for this look quite straightforward. After Moore bought the bare rolling hill country which became Glenmark, he put his men to the task of draining the swamps. They soon began to uncover bones of the giant moa, the huge herbivorous birds which weighed a quarter of a tonne — 250 kilograms — stood 3.6 metres tall at a stretch and once roamed over the plains and foothills of the island. The first moa bones found at Glenmark were stored in the woolshed, but there were so many they began to take up too much room.

In 1866 Moore invited the government geologist in Canterbury, Julius Haast, to come and see the aggregation. At the time, Haast was planning a museum for Christchurch. He drove away from Glenmark that day with a 'large American four-horse waggon' full of moa sub-fossils. This was a gift of enormous value. By then museums around the world all wanted a specimen of the 'wonderful, struthious bird', as it was called by Richard Owen, the famous naturalist who identified it in 1843 from a section of leg bone sent to England. (Everyone else thought the fragment must belong to a horse or an ox.) Haast began a brisk trade in his booty from Glenmark.

There was not much room in his workshop in the tower of the Provincial chambers in Christchurch, so Haast and his assistant, a taxidermist named Frederick Fuller, laid out their bony jigsaws on the grass between the Chambers and the Avon River, which slid gently, genteelly almost, through the centre of Christchurch, the pious if rather tipsy little town whose spires, turrets and lychgates, along with 34 pubs, had sprung up a few years before on the southern marches of Polynesia.

Arranged into sub-species and individual specimens, the skeletons were packed up and shipped to the museums of Europe, which in return sent items from their own holdings. 'Animals trooped in as they did for Noah,' Haast's son wrote. 'Birds of every hue, insects of every dimension, stone implements of the vanished races grouped themselves in historical train.'[2] Plaster casts of famous classical statues arrived as well — *Venus de' Medici, Diana Robing, The Dying Gladiator, Boy with Goose, Cupid and Psyche*. Within a few years Haast had a magnificent museum in the middle of town.

Meanwhile the wagons kept arriving from Glenmark.

Moore even put a team of workers at Haast's disposal to excavate the swamps, the 'precious bog' as it came to be called, and Haast's assistant, Fuller, was often on hand to supervise the proceedings.

One day in March 1871 Fuller, who with his 'flowing hair and beard looked like some figure of the Ober-Ammagau passion play',[3] looked into the bog and saw, lying there among the moa bones, a single huge claw, like a dagger at a pyjama party. He realised it had belonged to a raptor of immense size.

A few weeks later Haast held up the claw (above) at a meeting of the Philosophical Institute. There were gasps from the audience. 'Only the lion and tiger perhaps have larger ungual phalanges than this extinct raptorial bird,' said Haast, who had to assure one anxious member of the audience that its owner really had been an extinct bird and not some unknown giant feline still living in the mountains.

Haast went on: 'Having seen its curved talons, the fable of the bird Roc no longer seems so very extravagant and strange . . . I may add that a human being, if not well-armed or very powerful, not to speak of children, would have stood a very poor chance against such a formidable foe, if it had chosen to attack him.'[4]

Soon after this discovery, certain Māori tales were remembered which told how Māori who first settled the island had to do battle with a gigantic, beautiful and very dangerous bird, the Pouākai, which attacked human beings and 'carried them off' to feed its chicks. Ancient songs about a giant eagle known as Te Hōkioi were also set against the discovery at Glenmark. In the 1850s, Māori in the Whanganui district had informed the missionary Rev. Richard Taylor that an immense bird they called a Pouākai 'lives on the tops of the [South Island] mountains'.[5] The present tense was used.

Thinking the matter over, Haast began to wonder whether he himself might not have seen the eagle on his journeys into the interior of the South Island. He recalled a sighting in 1862: 'The most interesting inhabitant of these Alpine regions is a very large bird of prey of crepuscular and nocturnal habits which visited our camp first on the night of April 6 when we were sitting round the fire. For a short time we heard the flapping of its wings which became every second more audible. For a moment it sat down close to us but before we could reach the gun it rose and disappeared . . .'

Again in 1866 he saw a 'large bird of prey pursuing a sparrow hawk and flying very high above us', and for the rest of his life he remained unsure about these encounters. 'It is possible that the large bird of prey met with in the heart of the Alps may be . . . the *Harpagornis*, of which the bones were first discovered in the turbary deposits of Glenmark,' he wrote in 1879.[6] In London the celebrated Richard Owen declared himself 'charmed' by the 'gigantic raptorial' and in 1872 he read a paper on the subject to the Zoological Society, but even before that he wrote to the editor of *The Academy* magazine to break the news.

The discovery at Glenmark was not just of scientific importance. It had cultural and literary significance. It was a little late for Henry Yule's famous translation of Marco Polo's *Travels*, which had just been published, but in the second edition, of 1874, there it was: 'The bones of a veritable Ruc from New Zealand lie on the table of Professor Owen's Cabinet,' Yule wrote in his preface. *Harpagornis* had begun its strange career as a source for the ancient legend of the Roc, or Rukh, or Rukhkh, of Sindbad.

Haast meanwhile began a new international trade, this time in eagle claws — not real ones, as there was still only one of them available, but in plaster casts — which were sent in all directions, to London, Vienna, New York. It was the size of that terrible talon which made Haast think of the Greek *harpax*, a grappling hook, and provided him with the descriptive part of the name. At the Philosophical Institute that night in 1871 he concluded his speech: 'In order to pay a just compliment to my friend, Mr G. H. Moore, of Glenmark, who has always afforded me every facility in his power to pursue my researches, I propose the name of *Harpagornis moorei* . . .'

The grappling-hook-bird of Moore.

But it is an odd story. How to account for the unstinting generosity on the part of a man who hated his neighbours, cut off his wife and sons without a penny and cared nothing for public opinion? Among the facilities 'always afforded' to Haast was the woolshed which the swagman Henry Davis could not find on the last night of his life and which was then barred to him in death. Perhaps, in Haast, Moore had finally met someone to admire. He himself might walk 40 miles to town and sleep in a flax bush, but Haast had set about exploring the whole South Island, marching over mountain ranges in ten-league boots as if out on a morning stroll.

Haast's decision to honour Moore was also out of character. Meticulous, hard-working, generous and kindly, Haast was a leading figure in colonial society. He had been a lonely young outsider when he arrived from Austria and was delighted years later to find himself successful and famous and surrounded by ladies in Christchurch drawing rooms, and even more pleased when Emperor Franz Josef gave him a knighthood, which meant he could put 'von' in front of his name.

Haast, in other words, was a social lion, and these are often timid animals in one respect: they don't like to risk their status. Yet here he was saluting the outcast, whose hand the good people of Christchurch were advised never to clasp, and even bestowing a kind of immortality on him. Under normal protocols the eagle should have been named *Harpagornis fulleri*, after the taxidermist who first saw the claw in the bog and swiftly identified its owner.

Far away in London, Richard Owen thought so, and made public and rather pointed references to Fuller's part in the story of *Harpagornis*. Fuller was a likeable character, also hard-working and skilled, but easy going, tolerant, a father of seven, fond of a drink. He accompanied Haast on journeys into the

Alps, and Haast often paid tribute to the diligence and skill of 'Mr Fuller who has worked day and night indefatiguably [sic]'. The discovery of the eagle's claw was the climax of Fuller's career, but at that point Haast ignored him and turned instead to honour Moore of Glenmark.

Depressed perhaps at the injustice of the world, Fuller began to drink more heavily. Haast dismissed him for drunkenness. Fuller appealed to the people of Christchurch for a fair hearing but the newspapers would not publish his letter. In a fit of despair he ran to his workshop and drank from a bottle of taxidermist's arsenic. 'Oh Fred, I am poisoned,' he called to his son, and 'fell and rolled over in the yard'. He died two days later, leaving his family destitute.

If Haast had followed the usual rule this lamentable scene might never have occurred and the eagle would now be *H. fulleri*. There is a mysterious aspect to the names things bear. Some are eerily apt, as if fate itself has stepped in, and the point of the intervention seems to be that names matter.

'Names rise from the heart of a thing,' said Dante. It would be hard to think of an idea more thoroughly unmodern, yet in this case the great apex predator of the Southern Alps was named not after the mild taxidermist who looked like a figure from a passion play but after the pitiless and grasping runholder behind whose back the 'air turned blue' — a kind of apex predator himself who for a few years came to rule over the same rolling hills where the eagle once flew.

After Fuller's death, Haast was stricken by remorse: he immediately set up a collection of funds for the widow and gave her title to some of his own property so she and her children could keep a roof over their heads.

Chapter 2

One day in 1980, deep in a cave named Honeycomb Hill in the north-west of the South Island, a man named Phil Wood found the relics of a strange creature. There was a sinkhole nearby and it was in the dim light coming down from the forest floor that Wood saw the curve of a large bone, 'shaped like a spoon' he later told me, in a pile of spalled rubble.

Wood was not a scientist — he sold menswear for a living — but he was an experienced caver, had found cave fossils before and knew this one did not belong to any species which was living or, so far as he knew, had ever lived in the forests above his head. He decided to send it to the museum in Christchurch for identification.

The answer that came back was something of a riddle. What he had found, he was told, was the humerus or wing bone of *Harpagornis moorei*, commonly known as Haast's eagle, and although there had been much excitement when remains were found at Glenmark a century earlier, interest soon waned. Von Haast and Owen believed the eagle had hunted its prey, but in a fit of national modesty New Zealand scientists in the 1890s decided they were wrong and that *Harpagornis* was not a proper eagle at all, but a kind of flightless scavenger. Its sheer size was its downfall. Haast had noted that the major wing bone, the ulna, was 'relatively' short. In other words, although the bird was three of four times larger than a golden eagle, its wings were not three or four times longer.

Soon the 'relatively' was forgotten, and *Harpagornis*, whose stock had briefly soared so high, was brought sharply down to earth. If it could fly at all, it could not do so well. It could not therefore have hunted and killed prey. Then everyone lost interest in this unlovely creature, which had gone rustling from corpse to corpse for its next meal. No scientific papers were published on *Harpagornis* for the next 80 years.

Only two or three complete skeletons of the eagle had ever been found. One was sent to the Royal Museum of Scotland and promptly mislaid in the basement. Another was discovered in the 1940s by archaeologists working on a moa-hunter site on the east coast of the South Island. They put the skeleton in an old iron oven nearby, then forgot to go back and collect it.

This was roughly the information that came from Christchurch in 1980. The caves themselves, though, the message went on, sounded promising. A team from the museum would soon come over to see if there was anything of real interest in the area Phil was exploring.

What followed was a comical scandal later known as the 'raid' by Canterbury Museum. Perhaps museum scandals are inherently comic. A museum exists for a solemn and high-minded purpose, to bring some order to the slovenly archives of nature and art, but when a collection is put together in ways that don't quite bear scrutiny it is hard not to laugh. It took me some time to find out exactly what happened when the team from Christchurch arrived.

Thirty years later, Phil Wood, by then in his eighties, could hardly bring himself to talk to me about it.

'I was not happy.'

'About what?'

'What they did.'

'What did they do?'

'It wasn't what they did, it was *how* they did it.'

'How did they do it?'

'I was — not — *happy*.'

Interviewing Phil was not easy. He took early charge of the conversation but was naturally taciturn and touchy and could shut it down without warning. It was only when I contacted a scientist who worked for another museum at the time that I learned what had happened at Honeycomb Hill in 1980.

'Aha!' he wrote. 'I'd completely forgotten about the "raid" by Canterbury Museum . . . Phil Wood was very bitter about this, accusing them of simply grabbing everything interesting in sight, with no real thought to scientific exploration. He told us that they collected as many moa skulls as possible (these are far more rarely preserved than the larger leg bones of moa) . . . However, Phil told us that the skulls were often removed by the Canterbury Museum team from otherwise semi-complete skeletons and no proper notes of which skulls belonged to which bones were made at the time . . . Phil thought this very unscientific. (It was!).'

Once I knew Phil better, I realised it was not just the lack of scientific method that embittered him. He had been personally insulted. The visitors would never have behaved in such a way if other scientists or staff from another museum had been present, but there was only Phil Wood of Phil Wood Menswear, on the main street of Westport, and who cared what he thought?

Naturally Phil saw things in a different light. After all, Honeycomb Hill was not the first cave system he had explored, and *Harpagornis* was not his first find. There had been relics of the extinct giant goose *Cnemiornis calcitrans*, whose discovery caused quite a stir in palaeozoological circles, and what about the time he found the entire backbone of a whale lodged in a cave high in the hills above the Tasman Sea — a sight so extraordinary that the famous oceanographer Jacques Cousteau himself came to pay homage to the whale, and to greet Phil Wood as an equal.

On the other hand, what *did* it matter what Phil thought? The Canterbury visitors were leading figures in museum circles. They had published dozens of papers between them on their specialist subject, the moa. Who in the world knew more about the gizzard contents of the moa than they did? But they were archaeologists, not palaeontologists, and were mainly interested in that brief window in time when giant moa and human beings came face to face.

They hurried through the caves picking up skulls — these empty eye sockets might once have turned to the first human beings who set foot in the land! — and recording no data about where they found them. Phil Wood took them to the place where he had found the wing bone of the eagle and they picked up one or two other pieces of *Harpagornis* but they made it plain these were of minor importance. Then they went back to the surface and drove away laden with beaky treasure and were never heard from again.

Phil, for his part, went back to work behind the counter of his shop in the main street of Westport, a hundred-odd kilometres down the coast . . .

And there the story might have ended or remained on pause for another hundred years, but fate intervened in the form of a certain Dick Dell — Dr Richard Dell — who just then stepped on stage in a timely manner. Dell had recently retired as director of the National Museum in Wellington. His idea of retirement was to drive around the country looking for things to save. He arrived on the West Coast and happened to meet Phil Wood, who told him: 'I've got a cave full of bones no one's interested in.'

If Phil then mentioned the story of the 'raid' by Canterbury Museum, Dell would have been deeply shocked. He was a born conservationist. 'Put that boulder back' was a family motto. At the age of ten, he had opened his first museum (molluscs) in the henhouse in a backyard in Auckland. He listened carefully to Wood's account of the caves he had found and that no one cared about.

Meanwhile a new problem was emerging, in the form of an official known as the Assistant Conservator of Forests. Honeycomb Hill stands in the middle of a valley named the Ōpārara Basin. The land belongs to the state, and was then under the control of the Forest Service. The primary duty of the assistant conservator at that time was not, in fact, to conserve forests but to ensure the supply of timber for the nation's needs, and if not that, to make money from them in some way or other. The rainforest of the Ōpārara Basin had never produced a penny. Very well! Now it must pay its way.

It is hard to believe today some of the plans hatched by the Forest Service in the 1970s for the untouched bush on the West Coast of the South Island. First, the most valuable trees would be cut down and winched out for sale. Then exciting new technologies could be brought to bear. All the trees left standing would be bombed from the air with herbicides, with Agent Orange for instance, contaminated with dioxin, as used by the US Air Force to strip the communist-concealing jungles of Cambodia and Vietnam. The dying trees could be left to dry for about five years and then bombed again with an incendiary such as napalm, also used in Vietnam.

Poisoned, blackened and burned, the land would then be ready for a cash crop. In this case, pine trees.

It was the philosopher Thomas Hobbes who first advised humankind to 'make war on nature', our situation in the universe being so horrible, the argument ran, we might as well make ourselves comfortable . . . But not even gloomy-minded Hobbes could have imagined these weapons of war turned on a primaeval forest. After 40 years — in about 2020 — a local paper mill could be built and the pines of the West Coast turned into wood pulp.

The effect of deforestation on the caverns would be rapid and irreversible. Rainfall is high in the area. Heavy rain falling on bare hills would flood the labyrinth and debris would block the exits. All the strange and wonderful forms which rise from the floor and descend from the ceiling of limestone caves — stalactites, stalagmites, chandeliers, drapery and straws, fluted columns, frostwork and moonmilk crystals, rimstone pools, 'paddy-fields' and 'mushrooms' of micro-crystalline calcite — would be soon drowned and then dissolved by the acidity of the water. Fossils which had lain there for thousands of years would be washed away and lost forever.

The sound of chainsaws could already be heard approaching Honeycomb Hill.

Here now was a battle worthy of Dick Dell. This was something worth saving! Again, names seem to rise from the heart of the matter. *Dell* and *Wood* vs *Agent Orange* and *napalm*. But how would the battle be joined? Back in Wellington, Dell alerted museum staff to the existence of the caves, and Wood contacted them separately from Westport. Within a few weeks a second team of museum experts, this time from Wellington, arrived at Honeycomb Hill and Phil Wood led them down into the dark.

What they saw amazed them. Everywhere they turned their torches, it seemed, treasures lay half buried in fine red loam or grey fluvial silt. Taphonomy is the name given to the deposition of fossils. It has a soft footfall, this word, coined in Russia in the 1940s from *taphos*, the Greek for tomb or cave,[7] which suits the processes of fossil formation that take place unseen in silence and in darkness over many centuries.

Here, for instance, is a description of how *Harpagornis* fragments were preserved in one cave at Honeycomb Hill named Eagle's Roost: 'Throughout most of the time that these were accumulating [on the cave floor], powdery microcrystalline calcite speleothems grew on the surfaces of overhead roof and walls, and weathering resulted in a fine rain of red-brown loam derived from the impurities of the limestone . . . During heavy rain, percolation waters periodically flowed over the cave floor . . . so that fossils were gently worked into the matrix of loam and fine calcite . . . At Eagle's Roost, many bones of two different eagles were deposited on a central debris-cone which subsequently was eroded or dissolved away . . . The bones worked their way downward and laterally, so that the bones of the same bird ended up at least five metres apart, and one of these birds was only 16,000 years old.'[8]

Only 16,000 years old — that lovely 'only' sums up the vast periods that Time sets aside to make a fossil.

Other natural features made Honeycomb Hill an unusually rich site, taphonomically speaking. The caves have about 70 entrances: several are sinkholes which are just wide enough for a bird to fly into but not out of again (few species can fly vertically upwards) and which are also filled with sunlight at some point of the day. The waterflow is persistent but the stream which had carved out the upper chambers has long since abandoned them for the deeper galleries. The only result of later floods in the upper caves is to cover fossils gently with more silt. And there was no sign, in 1980, of intrusion by mammals — by rodents, for instance, which gnaw bones and scatter them, or human beings who pick things up and carry them away.

Honeycomb Hill, its dark halls and galleries stretching in all directions, was a kind of Grand Palace of taphonomy. A preliminary report was made for the National Museum in which the writer could hardly contain himself. Even this little mark — ! — rarely sighted in scientific documents makes an appearance. 'Honeycomb Hill is a tremendously exciting site . . . quite clearly of national, if not international importance . . . The state of preservation is quite outstanding . . . The bones of even very small birds have been preserved . . . 32 species of bird were recorded in this brief visit!'[9]

The visitors stayed at Honeycomb Hill for two days. Since time was short, Phil Wood took them only to places in the system where he had seen fossil deposits. On the second day he led them to the cave where he had found his wing bone in 1980. There, almost immediately, casually as it were, they found another. Despite *Harpagornis*'s fall from grace, the visitors were impressed, for eagle fossils were extremely rare. But then something even more impressive took place. They noticed a high shelf covered by an overhang of rock. One of them climbed and found the shelf covered with the bones of tiny songbirds — 'thousands of them!' he wrote to me years later — 'much smaller than matchsticks'.

One of the visitors was the museum's curator of birds, Sandy Bartle, who had a special interest in the Acanthisittidae, a family of birds as small as wrens, drab in colour, quite insignificant in appearance, but of the most illustrious lineage.

The Acanthisittidae belong to the ancient guild of song-birds. Singing is not a universal characteristic of birds and it was probably 'only' 70 million years ago (birds are thought to have evolved more than 100 million years ago) that an isolated group developed the polytonal syrinx, a voice-box with several muscles, allowing them to call in complex patterns.

For the first time in history birds began to sing.

This little group evolved in a part of Gondwanaland which later became the south-west Pacific but, equipped with song, they then spread out around the world, mastering almost all environments and taking innumerable new forms. Most of them are known, not very accurately, as the passerines. The word comes from the Latin *passer*, the sparrow. In the classical era a famous love song was written in Rome. *Passer mortuus est meae puellae, passer* sang the poet:

> My girlfriend's sparrow is dead,
> the sparrow of my sweet darling . . .
> Now he flies down the dark road to death
> from where they say no one returns.

Perhaps Catallus was only pretending to mourn. Was he jealous of the pet which was allowed to nestle so sweetly in Clodia's (or was it Lesbia's?) bosom? Stranger things have been known. For two millennia critics have objected to the way Catullus sends a sparrow fluttering down the famous avenue to the underworld.

Sometimes, though, there really is providence in the fall of a passerine. As soon as Sandy Bartle found the shelf covered with tiny bones he began work, delicately excavating fossil remains which in any other cave would have been swept away or degraded thousands of years earlier. Working with him was an avian osteologist named Phil Millener. Within a few hours they had found remains of four of the five known species of Acanthissitidae — the rock wren, the bush wren, the rifleman and the stout-legged wren. Then Bartle came across a little skull which did not belong to any of them, and Millener realised it belonged to an unknown species. Further fragments were found, a picture built up and later a name was given.

Dendroscansor decurvirostris was a little larger than the other wrens, had a longer bill and, to judge from the diminished keel of the breastbone, was flightless and ran fast like a mouse across scrubland rocks and forest floor. Here was a completely new member of the family of the Acanthisittidae, which had stayed home for 80 million years and hardly changed their appearance but were, in a way, the living ancestors of all the songbirds in the world.

This ended the threat to Honeycomb Hill. New Zealand is a young country and still turns to the natural environment — forest ferns and stars overhead — for its ID, so to speak, and proof of address. A new bird species, even one extinct for centuries and possibly never seen by human eye, is a kind of national treasure.

The assistant conservator knew he was beaten, or perhaps he had a change of heart. He had come on the trip to Honeycomb Hill out of curiosity, and to keep an eye on the enemy. He and Sandy Bartle had crossed swords previously over conservation of forest habitat. Seeing the importance given to the tiny songbirds, and especially to the unknown new specimen, he retired from the field, and the sound of chainsaws and the march of pine seedlings abruptly ceased in Ōpārara.

One day, in other words, a little wren fluttered down a sink-hole and couldn't get out again. That event, instantly forgotten in the song-filled forest above, 12,000 years later saved the caves of Honeycomb Hill, and the same song-filled forest, from destruction.

Chapter 3

Up to this point the history of the eagle — the modern story, that is, which began when Fuller saw the great claw in the swamp — has been reasonably straightforward. What happened next though, in the following decade at Honeycomb Hill, is rather mysterious.

On the surface everything looks simple. The caves had been saved. Teams of scientists and museum staff came and went from Wellington. Phil Wood continued exploring, naming and mapping the underground system. He had chosen the name Honeycomb Hill on account of its amazing complexity; eventually more than 15 kilometres of passages and galleries were found squeezed below 1 square kilometre of surface area. The apiarian theme stuck. Bees Knees. Buzz Avenue. Hives Passage. Hives Extension. The stream which had carved out the upper caverns and was still heard running far below was Honeycomb Flow.

New fossil discoveries began to generate international interest. In those ten years more than 60 species were found in the caves, many of them, including the tiniest, in an exquisite state of preservation. A BBC wildlife documentary maker was attracted by the stir, stimulating public interest. And yet there was a problem below ground. There was some kind of dissension, unhappiness, a contest of wills between Phil Wood and the museum staffers visiting Honeycomb Hill.

The only matter in dispute, as far as I could make out, was the status of *Harpagornis moorei*. Mighty aerial predator, or dismal flightless scavenger? Officially the question had been settled decades earlier, in favour of the scavenger, but for some reason Phil now took up the cause of the predator, against the young men from Wellington, who stuck firmly to the conventional scientific view. But 30 years on, if the matter was raised, the language of both sides was beautifully calm and diplomatic:

'*Our* interest,' one of the museum people told me, 'was in the beautifully preserved passerine bones. I think that Phil was a little disappointed we weren't more excited by the eagle finds.'

'*I* think,' Phil Wood said, 'they liked finding the smaller bones of the wren and one turning out to be a new species. But to me, *Harpagornis* was a symbol. *We had an eagle!*'

Only occasionally a few words were let slip which hinted at the real atmosphere below the surface at Honeycomb Hill:

'Phil's a bit crazy, you realise that?'

'Phil loves mysteries.'

'He's full of bullshit.'

'He sent us down a corkscrew cave until we got wedged in. It *wasn't funny!*'

No more information was forthcoming. Why did Phil adopt the cause of von Haast and Owen's true-flying eagle? I never found out. By the 1980s there was a little band of heretics, outsiders mostly — an amateur ornithologist, a student named Holdaway — who also believed in the great predator and who had begun to publish their ideas, but did Phil know they existed? My own guess was that he never recovered from the 'raid' by the visitors from Canterbury Museum. They had looked down their noses at *Harpagornis*. He would take up its cause! They had humiliated him in his own underground realm. This must never happen again. And here was Honeycomb Hill filled with more museum experts, who also took no notice of his opinions. Down into the corkscrew cave with them!

This is only guesswork, since 30 years later no one was talking, but it is clear that on the question of the eagle, one side was right and one side was wrong, and it also seems that among the side that was wrong were some who had their doubts and began to waver, and then an event took place that would settle the matter once and for all — an event not at Honeycomb Hill but about 50 kilometres across roadless forest on the summit of a great marble massif, Mount Owen, named by chance after Richard Owen who, a century earlier, had declared himself 'charmed' by *Harpagornis*.

One summer day in the last week of 1989, or perhaps the first week of 1990 — the records differ — a student named Dave Smith was hiking over Mount Owen, looking for entrances to the cave system inside the mountain. Smith was skirting around the edge of a wide grassy amphitheatre known as

Sunrise Basin when he saw an aperture in the rocks. He decided to abseil down but after about 12 metres the shaft ended in a small double chamber. Turning to go up again, Smith noticed a few bones in the rubble and slipped a few, the sternum and the skull, into his pocket. Back in Nelson, he showed them to a zoologist who worked for the National Museum.

The very next day a helicopter lifted off from Nelson airport and headed for the summit of Mount Owen. On the way the weather closed in. Rain hid the mountain and wind began to gust to 100 kilometres an hour but there was no thought of turning back. Here was another mystery. The zoologist in Nelson was one of those who had worked at Honeycomb Hill during the past few years; he identified the bones as belonging to *Harpagornis moorei* and he wanted to see the site *now*.

Yet, officially, nothing had changed. *Harpagornis* was still, according to scientific consensus, the lowly carrion-eater whose last-found skeleton was left in an old iron oven because no one remembered to go back and collect it, while the one before that was lost in a Scottish basement and no one could be bothered to go and look for it. And here was a helicopter clattering up through wind and rain to Sunrise Basin without a moment to lose, and the only new factor I could see in the equation was the personality of Phil Wood, as if it was his silhouette in the rain droplets around the little craft, urging it on . . .

The helicopter landed on Mount Owen and the two passengers abseiled down the shaft. It was just as the zoologist had guessed: scattered in the rubble was the skeleton of *Harpagornis*, complete almost to the smallest components, including even some of the scleral ossicles, tiny rings of bone which encircle the iris of the eye of some species, although not humankind.

This discovery at Sunrise Basin is said to have revolutionised the study of *Harpagornis moorei*.[10] The 'Mount Owen female', as the skeleton became known, was huge. First allometric readings gave her a weight of about 17 kilograms, about four times the size of a golden eagle. A complete overview of the body structure and proportions was now available. The heretics were re-energised. Close examination of the wing bones, the keel of the breastbone and the powerful legs and talons showed no signs of flightlessness or an inability to strike and kill. The pro-scavengers argued back in newspaper columns, but the public took no notice. It had decided, like Phil, in favour of the heroic. *We had an eagle!*

Meanwhile new technologies were coming to hand. In 2002 DNA was extracted from a bone of the Mount Owen female and from another fragment found in Otago, then taken to England and compared with samples from the toe-pads of a dozen species of 'modern' eagle. Among the data collected were these:

Little eagle: GTACATTGGACAGACCCTCGTAGAGTGAG-CCTGAGGCGGATTCTCCGTAGATAACCCC

Pygmy eagle: GTACATTGGACAAACCCTTGTAGAGT-GAACCTGAGGCGGATTCTCCGTAGATAACCCC

Haast's eagle: ATACATTGGACAAACCCTCGTAGAATGAG-CCTGGGGCGGATTCTCCGTAGATAACCCT

Completely meaningless to most people, this to a geneticist was written in letters of fire. Scientists construct a 'maximum-likelihood tree' to visualise how species are related. According to the DNA sequences, Haast's eagle, by far the largest of all eagles, sat on the same branch of the likelihood tree as two of the very smallest — the little eagle of Australia and the pygmy eagle of Papua New Guinea. And the differences between them were slight, meaning they had diverged quite recently.[11]

In other words, about a million years ago or perhaps more recently, a pair of little or pygmy eagles, or possibly one pregnant female,[12] was whirled more than 1600 kilometres across the Tasman Sea, probably by a storm or in a bushfire thermal (birds of prey do not usually choose to fly a long way over open water), reached the islands which are now New Zealand, and could not go home again. Their offspring then began to increase in size over time, competing against one another only in greed, and within several hundred thousand years they had grown at least ten times in size, by a whole order of magnitude, in the fastest change of morphology known in evolution.[13]

So that much was clear: *Harpagornis*'s little ancestors had been able to fly. But could their mighty descendants?

In 2008 a strange parliament of birds in skeletal from, including the Andean condor, the Egyptian vulture, the black vulture, the Australian wedge-tailed eagle and the white-tailed sea eagle, was assembled in the radiology departments of a hospital in Christchurch and another in Sydney, and wheeled in, along with *Harpagornis*, to undergo CAT scans — computerised axial tomography that spirals around a body bombarding it with rays which can peer into internal structures. A skeleton contains a good deal of information about the nervous system, which is partly hidden and protected by bone. The more a limb is used, for example, the larger the nerve supply it needs and the bigger the openings in the bone — the foramina — needed to admit the supply. By comparing the foramina of different birds, a CAT scan can show not only whether a species could fly but also *how* it flew — swerving fast like a falcon through a forest, for instance, or soaring like a hawk or vulture over open country.

First the wing bones of the assembled species were examined. The results were reported in the *Journal of Vertebrate Paleontology*: 'Our analysis of the neural canal area in Haast's eagle suggests . . . the eagle is closer to soaring and gliding Falconiformes or the Egyptian vulture and Andean condor than the smaller forest eagles . . . This does not preclude powerful wing muscles . . .'[14]

So *Harpagornis* could indeed fly, like its ancestors. But how did it live? Attention was turned to the legs and talons. Did the 'grappling hooks' of Haast strike to kill, or merely hop and scrabble over a corpse? The openings in the lower vertebrae through which nerves go down the legs to the talons are called the sacral foramina. In an eagle some of these are visible to the eye, but others — synsacral foramina five, six, seven and eight — can be seen only by a scan.

The machine was turned on again. CAT scan images have a spectral, half-starved look as if the machine is not quite sure what it is reporting, but in this case the dark holes of the sacral foramina, which look like flute stops or caves on a faraway cliff face, gave up their secret almost at once, and a million years of evolution was clear.

Sacral foramina five, six, seven and eight of *Harpagornis* were *ten times* larger than those of the Egyptian vulture or the Andean condor.

Haast's eagle had been a mighty hunter.

'Our analysis of the synsacral nerve roots suggest that the muscles and joints of the hindlimb were richly innervated with motor and/or proprioceptive fibres,' said the *Journal*. 'The talons of this bird were sensitive and powerful enough to grapple with live prey . . .'

That was the end of the controversy. The Māori legends were true. Phil Wood was right and the scientists had been wrong for a century. *Harpagornis moorei* was a kind of winged lion, huge in size, approaching the upper limit for flight, the apex predator in a complex ecosystem, swooping down to kill giant herbivores ten times its weight which roamed the forests and grasslands.

And these scenes had been witnessed by modern man, the first Polynesians to arrive, who, according to Māori, were also among its victims. There was no reason, after all, why the predator of a moa weighing 250 kilograms would not attack a bipedal stranger less than half a moa's height and weight, especially if the little newcomer was wearing a feather cloak.

The *Journal of Vertebrate Paleontology* does not normally retail tribal folklore, but in this case it provided two statements made by nineteenth-century Māori: 'This bird, the Hokioi, was seen by our ancestors. We (of the present day) have not seen it. The statement of our ancestors was that it was a powerful bird, a very powerful bird. It was a very large hawk. Its resting place was the top of the mountains; it did not rest on the plains. On the days in which it was on the wing our ancestors saw it; it was not seen every day as its abiding place was in the mountains. Its colour was red and black and white. It was a bird of (black) feathers, tinged with yellow and green; it had a bunch of red feathers on the top of its head. It was a large bird, as large as the moa.'

And this: 'A Pouaakai had built its nest on a spur of Tawera, and darting down from thence it seized and carried off men, women, and children, as food for itself and its young. For though its wings made a loud noise as it flew through the air, it rushed with such rapidity upon its prey that none could escape from its talons.'

That was the angle which took the fancy of the press. 'Maori legend of man-eating bird is true' was the headline I read one day in 2009 in London. I remember the moment clearly — late morning, a bright autumn day but the shadows were getting longer and from my room at the top of the house in Islington I could see the Shard half built on the horizon. I read the story with keenest interest. It was rare to see New Zealand on the front page of a British newspaper, and as well as that it is always satisfying to see science forced to acknowledge the authority of legend.

At the same time I felt oddly dissatisfied. *I should have written this story*, I thought, which is a response familiar to writers reading someone else on 'their' subject. Yet Haast's eagle was not my subject. I knew that it had once existed — a few years earlier I had written about a Māori boy who was kidnapped in the Taranaki wars of the 1860s and then brought up by the colonial premier and his wife; in the course of my research I noticed that a range of hills in the background of the story was named Pouākai, presumably after the eagle.

It even occurred to me that this Pouākai might be connected in some way to the Roc or Rukh of Arab legend, but since no one in the story of the kidnapped boy ever referred to the Pouākai in any way I let the matter drop. I knew so little about the species, in fact, that until that morning in London I had never realised that for a long time it was the subject of scientific contention.

But now that it came flying back into view so strongly on the front pages of the press, I was interested again. When I thought I should have written the story, what I really meant was this: something was missing. *There should be more.* For here, beyond doubt, was one of the great creatures of the world, quite the equal of the lion or tiger or elephant, or Behemoth or Leviathan or any of the charismatic beasts that move slowly above our heads in the zodiac of the night sky. Yet almost nothing was known about it. *Harpagornis* had no symbolic weight.

The golden eagle of Eurasia, for instance, in Western tradition alone, represents eloquence, armed force, power, the state, transcendence, St John the Evangelist, Zeus, the legions of Rome, England,[15] Napoleon's army, the Wehrmacht, and perhaps, by cousinly extension, the first American moon landing. Haast's eagle, on the world stage at least, symbolised nothing, except perhaps obscurity.

Even in Māori mythology it was oddly reclusive. The only reference to it that I had ever read was to the bird named Te Hōkioi, which was never seen but only heard, and only at night, and only rarely, in a time of danger, an ancestral voice warning of war. And even in that signal role it was often confused with another legendary night bird, the Hakūwai.

It is true that *Harpagornis* lived in the most remote country in the world and was seen only by a tiny number of people before it vanished, almost as they arrived, and probably because they arrived, yet creatures which are purely imaginary or long extinct have a place in the ecosystem of the imagination. The unicorn and the dragon prance across official stationery and on the tailfins of airlines. Children think vividly about the monsters of prehistory. *Harpagornis moorei*, it seemed, had never made it into the system. Or had it? Was it there after all, but hidden, or lost, or in disguise? Or had its 'meaning', its real symbolic value, not in fact been recognised yet?

Chapter 4

It was a year or two before I stumbled on an answer to these questions. I say 'stumbled' because I was not looking very hard — I was busy with other things, just finishing a book set in England and Michelangelo's Italy, and thinking about a new novel which had the Iraq war of 2003 in the background. I spent six months reading and trying to understand that war and why it had ever been fought. Everyone knew why it *wasn't* fought — to take weapons of mass destruction from the hands of the tyrant. That was the excuse or lie told by the US government to justify an invasion of Iraq but no one seemed to know or even care very much what it *was* about. 'Oil,' people said vaguely. 'Democracy. Human rights.'

It struck me that how a war is fought tells you more about why it was fought than anything the politicians say. You do not, for instance, reopen the torture chambers of the tyrant if you are invading his country to improve human rights. I found

myself staring at a news photograph of US Deputy Secretary
of Defense Paul Wolfowitz, tieless, jacket off, striding through
the new-painted halls of Saddam Hussein's most notorious
prison, Abu Ghraib, open for business again one bright day in
2003. What was Wolfowitz thinking?

The US took to torture by a curious route. Officially, the
Geneva conventions against torture were not set aside by
the US because they were quaint and out of date, as was the
case with the Gestapo, but for the opposite reason. The US
held the conventions in such high regard, according to one
analysis, that it would have been a travesty to allow them to
protect 'Arab terrorists'.[16] The Pentagon top brass was suitably
bamboozled by this argument, and America set off down the
path which disgraced its name. The screams heard in Abu
Ghraib, as various sadists set about torturing innocent citizens
of Baghdad, were proof that, in American eyes, the Geneva
conventions were *sacred*.

It was a relief to get away from this stuff now and again,
and drop back into the tenth century and watch Sindbad, for
example, another citizen of Baghdad, setting out from Basra
on his Second Voyage, on the way to the strange land where
he encountered the Rukh: 'We set sail and made excellent time
across the sea and Fate willed we should touch on an island
of great natural beauty, covered with tall trees, rich in fruit
and flowers, filled with the singing of birds, watered by cool
streams, but utterly uninhabited.'

Harpagornis, in other words, and a possible connection
with the Rukh of Sindbad, was still in my mind, at the back of
a queue — an odd but orderly queue which included certain
statues carved by Michelangelo, the US torture chambers in

Iraq, and a very large eagle in want of mythology.

I can't remember now exactly what sent me to the library one day to look for a book with the magnificent title *Exegisti Monumenta* ('You Have Measured the Monuments'). This was a collection of essays written by various scholars to mark the sixtieth birthday of Nicholas Sims-Williams, a specialist in the extinct languages of central Asia. Among the 40 articles, which include 'A Jewish Inscription from Jam, Afghanistan', 'A Sasanian Silver Bowl' and 'The Parthian "Sermon on Happiness"', is one entitled 'The Rukhkh, Giant Eagle of the Southern Seas' by A. D. H. Bivar, professor of Iranian studies at London University.

There was a French writer, a poet of the early twentieth century whose name now escapes me, who claimed he could tell if a book was any good just by touching the spine. Even as *Exegisti Monumenta* in its scarlet jacket was handed over the issue desk I knew it was going to be important. Of course the title alone of Bivar's essay conveys much information. It more or less states as a fact that the Rukhkh, or Rukh, or Roc, best known for terrifying Sindbad the Sailor on his Second and Fifth Voyages, had lived in the South Pacific. Since there were no other huge eagles in the region, the Rukh must have been *Harpagornis moorei*, or the Pouākai or Hōkioi of early Māori.

Bivar was not the first to propose the theory — it had occurred to many people; to Haast, for instance, as soon as he saw the great claw from the bog, and various nineteenth-century scholars such as Henry Yule, who edited Marco Polo's *Travels*. It had even occurred to me when I was writing about the kidnapped boy, but no one had taken the idea further. For them, as for me, it was just a passing fancy. Bivar, however, was not capable of passing fancies. He simply knew too much. I never met him — he died not long after I read his essay — but I saw his photograph on the internet and he had the look of a wise old bird perched at the crossroads, gloomily satisfied that the worst fears about humanity generally come true.

The 'crossroads of history' are the place where gallows are often set up. Bivar's main area of interest was that part of the world now encompassing Iran and Afghanistan, where transitory empires — the Kushan and Sasanian and Arsacid — rose and fell, along with shadowy kingdoms whose Zoroastrian, Buddhist and Greek remnants are still standing in lonely valleys if they have not been dynamited by the bearded vandals of the twenty-first century. Bivar specialised in the records of these cusps and twilights of history — Sasanian rock reliefs, Kushano–Sasanian chronology, Mithraic iconography, pre-Islamic folklore.

He begins his essay in *Exegisti Monumenta* with a list of the great winged raptors of ancient, classical and Islamic myth — the Griffin, the Anqa, the Rukh, the Simurgh of the Persians — and their probable forebears: the griffin-demons of ancient Assyria, and the Sumerian lion-headed eagle which stole the Tablets of Destiny from the gods.

These mythical birds originated in different cultures and at different times, but over the centuries they tended to crossbreed and merge, the Anqa, the Simurgh and the Rukh often becoming indistinguishable. It was in Bivar's gift to disentangle their lineages, and there was a simple insight at the heart of his essay: 'The Rukhkh always seems to have been located in the China Seas.' In Arab and Persian geography of the Middle Ages, 'the China Seas' meant the part of the Great Encircling Ocean which lies to the east of China: in other words the Pacific.

Bivar was also an authority on mediaeval Arab travellers, notably Ibn Battuta, who was the last of them and who sometimes almost seems modern. Ibn Battuta's account of a 42-day voyage in the late 1340s far out into the Pacific, where he thought he saw the Rukh, made a sighting of the New Zealand coast by earlier Arab mariners, and therefore an encounter with *Harpagornis*, seem feasible to Bivar.

He was careful to acknowledge the problems with the theory. The stories of the Rukh told by mediaeval travellers were subject to 'epic hyperbole' and a 'fog of hearsay and exaggeration', yet the new information from Honeycomb Hill and Mount Owen, he said, made it clear that such wild exaggerations should 'no longer be regarded as entirely divorced from fact'.

Other contenders for the home of the Rukh, such as Madagascar, were considered but discarded, for no particularly large eagle or bird of prey had lived there. The South Island of New Zealand was unique. 'It is my understanding that historians of New Zealand are generally sceptical of such visits,' Bivar writes, 'yet Arab accounts of the Rukhkh suggest that occasional visits of this kind did take place, since only there could a *veritable* giant eagle have been encountered'. My italics. Bivar was gently insisting on his point. After all, what did those sceptics know about the griffin-demons of south-west Asia?

Bivar was 83 when the essay was published. How much time he spent writing it is not known — 'a trifle', he called it — but he had spent decades accumulating the knowledge on which it was built, and his essay was edifying in the full sense of the word: it raised a great structure in the air, and it also supplied the absence I felt reading the newspaper story about *Harpagornis* in 2009. If Bivar was right, then the giant eagle seen long ago by only a handful of people in the remotest land in the world had nevertheless managed to take its proper place among the great beasts of the Earth and fly into the thoughts of millions of people in Asia, the Middle East, North Africa and eventually Europe.

Furthermore, it had done so before the land where it lived was settled, or perhaps even named, and then, much later, knowledge of the eagle even circled back to the place where it started, but now in disguise, so that when I was boy in Christchurch reading the tales of Sindbad in a children's version of *The Thousand and One Nights*, a copy I still have with its dark blue cover and alarming illustrations, it never crossed my mind that the Rukh in the stories might refer to a gigantic bird which had once lived just up the road, so to speak, in the foothills of the Southern Alps which, white with snow, could be seen on winter mornings from the outskirts of town, past the Ovaltine factory on the Main North Road.

But was Bivar right? His essay had made no waves, as far as I knew. And yet to state the whereabouts of Sindbad's Isle, where so many had travelled in mind over the centuries . . . Perhaps there was some flaw in the argument which I couldn't see. Perhaps, at only ten pages long and lacking a full chronology or details of the texts he cited, the essay was too slight to be taken seriously by scholars.

I re-read it, and for the first time noticed the name

Honeycomb Hill. There are about 60 million items in the British Library catalogue but only one has those two words in the title: *The Fossils of Honeycomb Hill*. This was a little book of 60 to 70 pages, not much more than a pamphlet, with silhouettes of moa and eagle claws on a light grey cover. It was written by a zoologist named Trevor Worthy, who had worked at Honeycomb Hill, and who was also — this was immediately clear — one of those rare beings: a scientist who can communicate well to ordinary readers on his specialist subject.

Before I had reached the bottom of page one, a vivid picture of Honeycomb Hill had come into mind: the Ōpārara Valley, hidden, windless, mild; the three great arches which stand over the river; the heavy rain falling on thick forest; and its strange crew of inhabitants — the great spotted kiwi, the two clever parrots, kea and kākā, the huge carnivorous snail *Powelliphanta*, a cave spider the size of a man's hand, which moves less than an inch in the course of its life — and the 'extensive moss cover which generates humic acids that stain stream waters a tea-brown colour'.[17]

For some reason the description 'tea-brown' had a strong effect on me. I was in the Rare Books Room in the British Library at the time. It was about midday. The walls of the library are too thick to let in the sound of traffic from Euston Road but I thought of the traffic outside and I thought of the Ōpārara River just then sliding under stone arches at midnight on the other side of the world, and I also thought that in about eight hours, when the library would be dark and closed, the sunlight of tomorrow would already be falling on the 'tea-brown' water. At that moment, under the high, white ceilings of the Rare Books Room, I made a sudden decision. *I'm going there*, I thought. And I also thought, though I didn't know why: *And if I'm going, I'd better get there soon.*

Chapter 5

Westport is the northernmost of the three main towns that contain most of the population of the West Coast of the South Island, and is the one that seems most cut off from the world. Highway 67 comes into town from the south and heads out again to the north with a fine air of assurance, but up ahead are only a few coastal hamlets and a scattering of dairy farms between mountains and sea, and soon the road begins to dwindle, then it loses the '67' and then it loses its tarseal and ends as a footpath disappearing into a forest, and although it is a very famous footpath — the Heaphy Track — a sense of cul-de-sac, the end of the line, seems to hang in the rainy atmosphere of Westport itself.

The main street is named Palmerston, after the British prime minister whose policies gave the world the term 'gunboat diplomacy', and this, I suppose, is one of the results: a mile or so of shops and pubs, wooden verandas over the footpath, a couple of banks, an Art Deco council chamber building of yellow bricks with two phoenix palms in front like brass candlesticks, and around the corner a grey stone war memorial twined about with red roses.

Parallel to Palmerston Street is a sleepy brown river and a wharf where fishing boats tie up, and at the far end of town is a great, grey, thundery beach littered with driftwood — driftwood on a heroic scale — where the Tasman rolls in, the rough 'male' sea in the Māori account, as opposed to the more serene and 'female' Pacific on the eastern coast.

I had kept the resolution I made in the Rare Books Room, although seven or eight months passed before I arrived in Westport on my way to Honeycomb Hill. I was travelling alone and it was late in the afternoon. I found a motel and was away out of town at dawn, the only signs of life I saw in the first hour of the day being two mottled black shapes — blackbirds hopping on the lawn behind the motel — which I saw through the bathroom window. No one was about when I drove through the streets and there was no traffic going in either direction on Highway 67 or in the little coastal settlements — Granity, Ngākawau, Hector — perched above the surf and the black shingle beaches still in the shadow north of Westport.

As the road went inland and climbed up around high forested bluffs, the prospect of sunrise seemed if anything to diminish: on that coast the rising sun has to surmount a wall of high eastern hills, and the further north you go, the closer the hills come to the road and the longer the sun is delayed. It wasn't until the road came back to the coast that the first beams struck over a hill and suddenly everything was brilliant, newly minted, light sparkling on cobwebs and on the drenched toetoe and reaching into the hollow of green waves falling on printless sand.

Ah, to be away down the backroads of New Zealand on a summer morning, far from the smoky continents of the north! I must have been ahead of a school bus by then, for every mile or so there now stood a child by a gate, or two children, prim, pink, schoolbags ready, scrubbed looking as if just down in the last shower. I crossed a one-way bridge over a wide tidal river and came into Karamea, the northernmost settlement on the coast. Karamea had an old-fashioned New Age look to it — there was a rainbow painted on the side of a barn, the word *organic* was written on high here and there, and the café on the main street had an elfin air, with garden tables and chairs in the shape of toadstools.

It was now 8.30. The café was shut — the elfin all still evidently abed — but the post office was open, and the Four Square store next door, and sturdy seniors in woollen jumpers were marching in and out, their four-wheel-drives parked haphazardly on the highway, Karamea presumably having no resident cop. Or perhaps he was still asleep, like the elfin. Or even — I once lived in small country town like Karamea — with the elfin.

I didn't stop; I was in a hurry now. Eight months late, I remembered the injunction in the Rare Books Room — 'You'd better get there soon' — and I drove on through Karamea, passed a few more dairy farms and was soon back by the sea: it was a lovely, high-mettled sea with driftwoody silver swells, and though I was in a hurry I didn't want to lose sight of it, even when I came to a sign pointing inland to Honeycomb Hill, and I carried on up the coast a few more miles until I saw a small cloud out to sea and so low above the breakers that it took the sidelong beams of the sun directly and was all lit up as if by internal filament. This struck me as a good omen, and I turned around there in the shingle and went back to the Honeycomb Hill sign, turned left and drove inland.

Then about a mile from the coast I saw another little cloud in front of me, just above the first high hill, and this time the sun was directly behind it so it was also all lit up from within. This I took as a *second* good omen, although I should have realised that two identical good omens in about ten minutes are of less value than one — the procession of low, rain-bearing clouds coming in off the sea is almost endless in that district and they weren't really omens at all, just the prevailing weather. But I didn't know that then and felt in good odour with the planet as I drove on into the bush, trees towering on both sides and the clean rainy scent of forest decay coming into the car like the smell of prehistory.

Then the road began to twist and turn so much I lost my bearings and had no idea which direction I was heading when I came out on a narrow saddle with a view on one side. I stopped the car and stood looking down into a wide forested valley. It was still dark below, the tallest trees sashed with white mist and birdsong reaching the road as if it was not only still dawn but always going to be dawn down there, and on that account alone I had a feeling I was looking at the Ōpārara valley I had read about in the Rare Books Room, and that the escarpment in the centre might be Honeycomb Hill itself, but I wasn't sure until I drove on a few more kilometres and came down a final switchback road to a carpark with signposts, a toilet block and a row of information boards . . . This was not at all the magical place that the name 'Ōpārara' had suggested but I knew Honeycomb Hill had been narrowly saved from destruction and the price was fame, and fame brings visitors who need angle parking and glassed-in information boards. On the other hand, it was now about 9.30 and no one else was there. Perhaps I would have the place to myself that day.

I parked the car and walked down the bank and there it was — the tea-brown river I had read about 22,000 kilometres away.

But it was just a little river babbling over rocks in the morning light. I walked upstream along the bank for 50 metres. I looked across the water and saw the interior upholstery of a moss forest, deep green and thickly piled. I felt rather foolish. Why had I come all this way? I was glad at least that I was alone — I didn't have to try to explain to anyone the impulse that sent me.

But just a few yeards further on, I looked up and saw a tremendous aerial cornice, maybe 25 metres high, festooned with ferns and epiphytes like a Piranesi ruin. This was such a surprise it reminded me of the first glimpse I ever had of the Sistine ceiling, which was so high and covered in earthy colours that it seemed like a work of nature rather than art, just as the great arch above me now seemed more a work of art than of nature, like the framework or setting of a story I couldn't quite read yet.

This, I realised, was the uppermost part of the middle of the three arches over the Ōpārara River, and I began to think perhaps it wasn't a mistake to have come here after all. I decided to walk on upstream to see the first of the arches, which I thought, from what I remembered of a pamphlet I had read in Westport, was about a twenty-minute walk away. The muddy track now left the river and led into the bush, but then the way was barred. A padlocked gate. A notice forbidding unauthorised entry — Site of Special Scientific Interest it said, or something to that effect. I thought about jumping the gate and carrying on along the track which led into deep bush but the idea of meeting someone in authority — the idea of Authority at all among those primordial trees — depressed me and I turned back, deciding instead to go downstream to the third arch, about a kilometre away. The mist was lifting now, in patches of gauze, and the mild suffused light in the valley was becoming brighter.

I heard voices. Ahead of me on the path was an elderly couple in green anoraks, festooned with cameras and camera gear. We stopped to talk. They were German — he was a professor although I forget what subject he said he taught, and his wife was a photographer who had come to photograph the arches. I heard motorbikes in the distance and hurried on. There were three bikes in the carpark and three Englishmen in black heavy-metal T-shirts were consulting the noticeboards. They seemed in a gloomy mood and the one nearest me did not return my greeting and carried on reading the history of logging in the district.

I went on downstream and came to the third arch. This one was low and massive, and also crowded with ferns, like people leaning over a bridge at a regatta, and there, standing by the tannin-darkened water looking up at the ferns and the great low roof above me, I remembered why I was there. I'd had an inkling of it in the Rare Books Room and needed to visit the place just for a few minutes, just to check. It was not so much to see whether the Ōpārara was the place where a book on the eagle, if there was to be a book on the eagle, should start, but the other way around. If it was as Trevor Worthy described it — the hidden valley, the ancient forest, the great arches over a dark river slipping out on its way to the sea ('ōpārara' means 'opening out') — then that in itself might be taken as a sign that Professor Bivar was right, and that the story of the eagle, which restarted here after a hundred years' pause, had indeed flown out halfway around the world and into the records of the great civilisations of Asia and the Middle East, which could be consulted under the high ceilings of the British Library.

I turned and went back up through the scrub towards the carpark. The sun was hot now: the mist had all gone and the last bellbirds, which love the dawn, had stopped singing. I could hear children calling through the trees instead and there were more cars coming down the switchback road. I didn't mind that now. I had found what I had come for. But I had been wrong about one thing back in the Rare Books Room. It wasn't a case of getting here *soon* but getting here *early* — before anyone else arrived, just to have a glimpse of the place as it was in 1980 when Phil Wood saw the curve of bone in the light coming down a sinkhole in the forest floor, and maybe even as it was thousands of years ago when the eagle in question had flown down the same sinkhole and couldn't fly back up again.

Chapter 6

Phil Wood I met a year later when I found myself, slightly to my surprise, back in Westport. After leaving Honeycomb Hill I spent the next few months reading anything I could find about *Harpagornis*, and although there were many places a book on an eagle that evolved a million years ago might begin, I still had that moment in my mind: when Phil first saw the bone in the cave, Honeycomb Flow sounding in the distance below.

Since I wanted to start with him, and had talked to him several times by phone over the ensuing year, it would have been odd, I thought, not to meet him in person. This time I was not travelling alone. I remembered the silvery swell of the sea and the narrow shingle road leading north towards the Heaphy Track and persuaded some friends and family members to come with me up the same road and walk at least part of the track. In the end seven of us set off along the footpath into the forest of nīkau palms and walked for three days. For three nights we heard kiwi begin to call at sunset, or rather at starlight, although not at the appearance of the first star or second or third but at that moment when there were suddenly too many to count — a triumphant, a jubilant cry it is as well, as though kiwi have no intention of falling extinct — and why should they, since there are too many stars to count?

On the fourth morning we walked out again and that night were back in Westport, dining on steak and red wine (we'd had to carry dried food on the tramp) and the next morning the party split up, some flying out and others driving to catch the Picton ferry, while I went downtown, parked beside the brown river and went to find Phil Wood of Phil Wood Menswear on the main street.

I felt some misgivings as I walked towards the blue awnings of his shop which I had spied out the night before. My conversations with Phil had been difficult and each one seemed like a new test in which I got a lower mark. We had started off well enough on the first call. Phil was pleased to talk about his underground discoveries and his early life. He was born in Westport, he said, went to school in Westport, first at Westport Primary, then Westport North, then Westport Technical. He took up scouting as a boy, and in 1947 went to a scout jamboree in France.

While we talked there was a clatter of pots and pans in the background.

'That's my wife, Margaret,' said Phil. 'Margaret! What's the name of that place in France I went to for the scouts?'

More saucepan clatter.

'Not *Paris*,' he cried. 'It starts with an M.'

Crash bang went the pots.

'M!' Phil declaimed. 'O! I! F! No. Not F! S!'

We arrived by degrees at Moisson, 80 kilometres north of Paris, where the first international jamboree was held after World War II, the *Jamboree du Paix*, famous for the dust clouds which roiled through the camp and an enormous rubber globe of the world which was sent rolling from time to time over the heads of the boys — 40,000 of them gathered in from all the recently warring nations. Back home in Westport, Phil went into menswear.

'How long have you been in menswear?'

'Sixty years!'

'In the same shop?'

'*Two* shops,' he cried, though it wasn't clear whether he meant two shops at once or one after the other. Meanwhile, he had kept up the scouting. He became a scout master, leading the older scouts, the Venturers, deep into the bush, and in 1976 they went into the wilds of the Ōpārara where no one liked to go alone in those days, he said, even though the tough hunters and trappers avoided the limestone country, the karst land, with its grikes and flutes and sinkholes down which a deerstalker might fall and never be seen again.

'I knew the caves were there,' Phil shouted. 'It was just a matter of getting in and finding them.' I had the impression the Venturers were taken by the scruff of the neck and marched into karst country whether they liked it or not.

Having penetrated the caves, Phil then began exploring, naming and mapping. I liked the names he had chosen. There were occasional deviations from bees-and-honey. Wren Wrecker. Deer Drop. Star Draught.

'Why did you call that cave Star Draught?' I asked.

There was a pause. Was he being accused of a poetic streak? That might not be welcome in a town like Westport.

'We could see the stars,' he shouted. 'It was draughty.'

Then we came to the moment when Phil found the wing bone of the eagle. This was what I was after. This was the moment, as I saw it, when the tale of the eagle began to take flight again. What were Phil's thoughts at that juncture? What did he *see*?

'I saw a big bone shaped like a spoon.'

'And what did you think?'

'First off, I thought it might be a goose.'

'A goose?'

'We once found some fossils of the giant goose and I thought this might be another one but of course as soon as I had a look at it, I knew it wasn't a goose.'

'And where was this? Where were you exactly in the caves?'

There was a pause.

'I'm not telling you,' he said.

'Oh.'

I waited for a moment.

'Can you tell me why?'

'I'm not telling you,' said Phil, 'and I'm not telling you why.'

This was the pattern of all our communications: a flying start, some interesting information and then a sudden disjunction, the sound of a door being slammed.

I remembered this as I walked along Palmerston Street towards the blue awnings, and at the same time the remarks of some of the museum folk who worked at Honeycomb Hill in the

1980s came back to me — *Phil loves mysteries. Phil sent us down a corkscrew cave.* And so it came as a pleasant surprise to walk into Phil Wood Menswear and finally spy — it was a big shop, crammed with merchandise and at first no one seemed to be around — in the furthest corner, behind a very wide counter, a mild and beaming patriarch, white of beard and blue of eye.

'Phil Wood?'

'Yes.'

'I'm Peter Walker.'

'Yes, that's right,' said Phil in an encouraging tone.

'I'm just passing through. I thought I'd call in and say hello.'

'That's right.'

'But if you're busy . . .'

'No, no! Margaret can take over. I'll take you back home and show you some of the stuff I've got.'

He picked up the phone and made a call.

'Peter's here,' he said.

I couldn't help admiring this performance. Like a conjurer, without lifting a finger, Phil had taken full charge of the situation — he had kindly confirmed my identity, made it plain my arrival was no surprise, and not only that — I was a familiar subject in conversation: 'Peter's here.'

Margaret arrived almost immediately, as if also by magic, although she had driven across town. She was tall and clear eyed and had been a great beauty, I guessed. She had an air of invincible calm as if she had decided long ago that patience, of all the virtues, was the one that would serve her best in life with Phil. She took his place behind the counter and he and I left the shop and got into her car, which was parked just outside on Palmerston Street.

Palmerston Street, meanwhile, was in the process of disappearing. I had been in the shop only five or ten minutes but in that time a dense summer fog had come creeping up from the river — the Art Deco council chamber was already lost to view, and the phoenix palms in front of it, and all the hues of main-street commerce — Toyland, One-Stop Photos! — were fading to a wintry grey. Yet the air was warm.

Phil made a stately three-point turn across the bows of main-street traffic and we came to the intersection with Highway 67. Looking across the road I saw one of my friends peering into a shop window. Jim Clad had come on the Heaphy Track with us and was to drive back with me over the Alps to Canterbury that afternoon. He had come down to Palmerston Street to go shopping, wanting to buy a present for his wife. A bracelet of local greenstone, he thought, would be an acceptable gift for Aurora back in Washington DC. But the shop he was looking in was closed and the fog was almost upon him.

'There's my friend from America,' I said to Phil. 'Do you mind if he comes along?'

Phil looked shaken at this change to his plan, but he stopped on the corner and I went over and called Jim, who came back and climbed in the front of the car.

'Aha,' said Jim, shaking Phil's hand. 'I see you've fallen in with bad company.'

'*What?*' said Phil.

'You know — running around town with the wrong crowd,' said Jim.

It was only merry American banter, but the effect was disastrous.

'Just what I'm starting to think myself,' said Phil grimly, and in the rear-view mirror I saw his expression change — rueful now, and bitterly satisfied, as if thinking *There, I've done it again* — *vipers in my bosom!* and a black cloud seemed to descend on us as we drove through the oddly treeless streets. Westport, surrounded by ancient forest, seems averse to an avenue on principle.

We stopped outside a flat-roofed bungalow. Phil led us around the side of the house to the backyard where there was a single apple tree — quite leafless, although it was still high summer — and in the back door. Once inside, the atmosphere improved. Phil's mood lifted as he laid out various press cuttings and cave curios and rock samples on the dining table. Then there was a long phone conversation with Margaret on a technical question — how to get the video player working.

I looked around. It was the home of an elderly couple; I recognised the brown velvet sofa and floral carpet of my parents' house 40 years before, and the patina, which old eyes cannot see, around light switches and door handles as if the native earth is quietly coming indoors early. There were apples everywhere, all rather spotted and wrinkled — apples on plates and in saucers and bowls on the sideboard and kitchen windowsill.

Phil rang off and the video came on. Even that had an antique look, the greeny-orangey hues of 1970s film stock. Now quite cheerful again, Phil gave us a running commentary, naming the caves he had found or explored — the Fenian, the Charleston, the Metro — the cave spiders he had seen, as big as dinner plates, and the huge kiwi, 'three feet high!' — he put his palm out flat at waist height — which had gone running past him in the rain. And suddenly there on screen were Phil Wood and the famous oceanographer Jacques Cousteau, leaning together in a cave, and then a second shot of a kind of notched white archway in the dark just above Phil's head.

'What's that?' I asked.

'That's a whale.'

'A *whale*?'

'It's the backbone of a whale.'

I had a general idea by then — I had grasped the principle — of how limestone and limestone caves are formed, but it wasn't until that moment that I realised the scale, the sheer grandeur — chords of Beethoven came to mind — of the operation. Aeon after aeon of marine organisms sinking to the sea floor, eventually forming a rock substrate which is then slowly lifted by tectonic forces towards the sunlight and out into the air and then, amid sidereal delays, higher and higher to form hills and mountains, all the while conveying the remains of the marine organisms which had formed it, even the very largest, even a whale, for instance, whose backbone might reappear in the wall of a cave carved out millions of years later by a river or by rain — a cave into which other life forms, much more recent (although themselves perhaps now extinct) might make their way, and die and also turn into fossils. Later still, more visitors make an appearance, such as Phil Wood and Jacques Cousteau, flickering in the video across the floral carpet in Phil's sitting room.

The whale whose spine hung in the dark behind them, bevelled like a Romanesque arch, had lived 40 million years ago — such a vast distance from today that the extinct eagle, by comparison, whose wing bone Phil Wood found, was virtually our contemporary; we had only just missed it, so to speak, flying above the leafless apple tree I could see out the window in the fog which had now arrived in Phil's backyard.

The video came to an end. Phil then brought out a map of Honeycomb Hill and unrolled it on the carpet. It was an impressive article — four sheets of architects' blue-grey drafting paper stitched together, stiff, dimly translucent and rattling to the touch. This was Phil's own handiwork. No other map of the caves, he said, had been made on this scale. A chart of a limestone cave system looks, for good reasons, like an ink blot or a water stain.

I realised I had another chance to ask Phil about the moment when he had found the wing bone. I roughly knew the location by then, from other conversations, but it would be good to hear it from Phil himself. Nearly a year had passed since he rebuffed me on the question. Perhaps he had forgotten his objections.

'So where are we?' I said casually, looking at the map. 'Can you show me on this where you were when you found the eagle in 1980?'

'I can,' said Phil. He challenged me with a stare. 'But I'm not going to.'

'Oh,' I said. 'Well, I mean, okay. Maybe it doesn't matter. I think Canterbury Museum has already let me know.'

'*Canterbury Museum*!' cried Phil. 'Canterbury Museum can tell you what they like but *I'm* not telling you.'

'Never mind,' I said quickly. What a blunder, to mention Canterbury Museum! I tried to move on.

'Anyway,' I said, 'tell me, what went through your mind when you first saw the bone? Didn't you think it was a goose?'

'A *goose*?'

His stare was now terrible.

'Sorry,' I said, 'I thought you said—'

'I *never* thought it was a goose,' said Phil. 'I knew that it *wasn't* a goose.'

'Sorry—'

'A *goose*?' Phil said again in disgust, and at that moment he seemed to grow in stature in the brown sitting room and look down at me with a gloomy and penetrating eye, like a judge at the moment of sentencing. I now bitterly repented of the goose, but it was too late. I had been judged and found wanting. Behind Phil I could see Jim on the sofa. He mouthed the word 'goose' and shook his head sternly. He was enjoying this.

Phil pounced on the great map and rolled it up, rattling it furiously. This, I was pretty sure, marked the end of our meeting. I left the room for a minute — maybe things would calm down — and went down the hall to the bathroom. On the way back I noticed all the wedding photos on the wall. There were so many in fact that they had spread out of the sitting room, around the corner and down the hall, and I vaguely saw now the algebra of the apples: the more children who left home, the more wedding pictures arrived framed in silver or gilt on the wall and the more the apples piled up in bowls and saucers, far too many in the end for one old couple to eat.

'Are these all your kids?' I asked, coming back into the sitting room.

Phil grunted.

'How many children have you got?'

'Seven.'

'Seven!' I said. 'And all gone now? All left home?'

No answer. I was trying to win him back of course, but he was having none of it. The interview was definitely over. We were ushered from the house and driven in silence back to town. Phil dropped us by the war memorial and drove away, and Jim, who had been a journalist once, began to laugh.

'Boy, you really messed that up.'

'I know, I know,' I said. 'That bloody goose . . .' And we both stood there laughing, although I was feeling rueful, and self-accusing. I *had* messed up. Canterbury Museum! A goose! I had steered straight for the rocks. I was a bad interviewer, and now there were things I would never know. Why had Phil taken up the cause of the true-flying eagle, against the whole scientific establishment? Was it bitterness at the 'raid' by Canterbury Museum? Had he won over any of the young scientists from Wellington? Was that the reason the helicopter flew through wind and rain to the top of Mount Owen without a moment to lose?

I felt almost in sight of a parable here: if Phil had been less touchy, if the Canterbury team had behaved better, he may never have taken up the eagle's cause, the story would not have taken off again, and I would never have arrived in Westport to be thrown out of his house and left standing on the footpath by the war memorial, with a strong sense of still being in the dark as the summer fog lifted around us.

Later that week, after driving over the ranges with Jim Clad, it occurred to me that Phil had in fact given me more information than I had realised. When he loomed over me in the brown sitting room I felt the full force of a powerful personality — easily angered, suspicious, fond of mysteries, yet with a kind of grandeur to him. Father of seven, finder of hidden things, namer of names, he was the type a much younger man (although as a scientist he could never admit it) might wish to please, or placate, if not propitiate.

And there was another reason a young scientist might have come around to Phil's point of view. On the question of the eagle, Phil was right and the others were wrong, and perhaps some people, especially if they are clever and thoughtful, like Trevor Worthy who wrote *The Fossils of Honeycomb Hill*, and who *was* the zoologist, I later found out, who booked the helicopter, know when someone is right and someone else is wrong, even if they don't know they know.

II

In Canterbury

Chapter 7

A few days after Phil Wood left us standing on the footpath in Westport, I was on the track of the eagle again, this time driving out of Christchurch towards the Southern Alps where, in 1862, Julius von Haast thought he saw *Harpagornis moorei*. It was not the hope of seeing another that sent me out of the city at eight on a hazy Saturday morning, but the story of the Pouākai that 'built its nest on a spur of Tawera, and darting down from thence . . . seized and carried off men, women, and children, as food for itself and its young'.[1]

Of all the legends I had read about the eagle in Māori or any other tradition, this was the only one which stated an actual location and I thought I should go there, just to stand on the hill and imagine myself a little closer to the subject. But where was Tāwera? It took me some time to track this down because the Māori name is no longer in use, and I was surprised eventually to find out that of the thousands of hills and mountains in New Zealand, Tāwera was already almost familiar to me, being one of the peaks in a cluster of high foothills named the Torlesse Range at the edge of the plains west of Christchurch.

I was driving out of town that morning with an old school friend — he could hardly have been older in fact, since Paddy McMahon and I first met aged five, at primary school; I have a clear memory of standing outside the school gate one afternoon with Paddy and his brother Terry, who was seven, and a boy named Eugene Terina, discussing world affairs. 'The Russians and the Germans,' Terry told us with a solemn air, 'really hate each other.' I was thunderstruck at this. I knew vaguely that such people as the Russians and the Germans existed, but that they had a collective opinion of one another and that Terry McMahon knew what these were — I was greatly impressed.

Possibly it was there, by the high, dark, dust-exhaling macrocarpa hedge at the school gate on Windermere Road, that I saw an early signpost to a career in foreign news which would take me to the other side of the world for many years. Paddy, on the other hand, stayed in Christchurch all his life, and had the benefit of an intimate knowledge of the people, streets, moods and stories of a single place, which I never experienced. As a young man he joined a mountaineering club and had climbed all over the Southern Alps and he knew Tāwera well, or rather the Torlesse Range. He was happy to take me there and show me around.

'What are we looking for exactly?' he asked, picking me up that morning from my cousin's house in south Christchurch.

'I'm not sure.'

'Will we know it when we see it?'

'Maybe not.'

'Aha,' said Paddy, happy to be off on a writer's wild goose chase, while pleased as well that he himself had a sensible profession.

This was the first time I had been in Christchurch since the great earthquake of 2011, which killed nearly 200 people and destroyed half the city, and as we drove out of town I found myself looking around for signs of damage, but it had been a very selective quake, Paddy said, smashing up mainly the poorer suburbs on the east side of town, and the oldest and most beautiful buildings in the centre — a very neoliberal quake, in other words — while our route took us through the largely undamaged western suburbs and we could have been in any city in the world on a Saturday morning, traffic just picking up on the way to the airport and DIY stores and garden centres on the edge of town. I was almost pleased finally to spy one old brick building with windows boarded up, grass on the sills and saplings on the front steps, but this, it turned out, was not a casualty of the earthquake but a former Catholic orphanage which had been closed in an abuse scandal.

'Some bad stories out of *there*,' said Paddy, and as we drove out of town he told me about a meeting he had been to, organised by the church to achieve reconciliation between the orphans, now all middle aged, and the nuns, now all elderly or very old, who had looked after them.

It was a miserable, bad-tempered occasion, said Paddy, who was there because his accountancy firm was involved in some way with the money the church had agreed to pay the victims. Some of the orphans were angry because they wanted more, and some of them thought that others had got more than their fair share, while a third group was unhappy that any money was being paid at all, saying the stories of abuse had been whipped up for financial gain. Meanwhile the nuns, old and doddery, some of them wheeled out of nursing homes, seemed to have no idea what was going on — or pretended they didn't.

Then one woman stood up at the back of the room and spoke.

'She hadn't said anything before,' said Paddy, 'but she had this strong, clear voice and she said just one thing and sat down, and then a complete silence fell.'

'What did she say?'

'She said, "There *was* abuse. The older orphans abused the young ones."'

'Oh,' I said. 'I never thought of that.'

'No,' said Paddy. 'Nor did I.'

'So the nuns were in the clear?'

'No, not necessarily,' said Paddy.

'So what happened?'

'Nothing,' said Paddy. 'What could happen? The orphans weren't all going to start suing each other, and the deal with the church had been done and the money was being dished out. But I was interested in that silence. It took me a while to work it out, but I think I know what it was.'

'What was it?'

'It was the *ring of truth*.'

'What do you mean?'

'It's what happens when someone says something that's true but no one has ever said it out loud before.'

'Oh,' I said. 'I hadn't thought of that either.'

We drove on in silence ourselves for a while and then started talking about other things, but I was also trying to remember a story I had heard which reminded me of the one Paddy told. It took a while to come back to me, and although it had happened a long time ago and I was not present, it had still managed to have an effect on my life. It was a story about a lynching in the United States. It was a particularly well-known lynching because a photographer had arrived just after the murders and taken a picture.

This was in Marion, Indiana, in 1930. In the photograph two young black men are hanging from a tree. There is an excited mob below them, men and women, old folk and young lovers, and some are pointing at the bodies and others grinning at the camera with expressions close to idiocy, as if cruelty made the mind as defective as it did the soul. This image was later seen by a Jewish school teacher, named Abel Meeropol, in New York, who wrote a poem and put it to music. The famous song 'Strange Fruit', which compares the bodies of lynched black men to a crop growing on southern trees, had come into being.

The song was picked up and recorded by Billie Holiday in 1939. It was sung by Nina Simone in 1964 and in a way was a background anthem of the whole civil rights movement in the 1960s. And then, in the mid-1990s, long after you might expect any new developments, more information came to light.

It turned out there had been not two victims that night in Marion but three. The crowd that came smashing into the jail took them away one by one. The first two were beaten and castrated and their bones were broken; one was dead before he was strung up. Then the mob came back for the third, a boy named James Cameron, aged 16. All three had been accused of the murder of a white man, and then rumours swept through Marion that a white woman, who was with the victim at the time, had been raped. This was a charge against black men so serious that white Americans were often content to kill the accused without any assessment of facts.

What had happened was this: the three young men decided to rob someone, to 'stick 'em up', and they went out to Lovers' Lane on the edge of town. A courting couple was targeted, but then young Cameron recognised the male victim and fled. After he had gone, the man was shot dead. All three of the gang were soon captured. The next day the shooting victim died and the woman alleged she had been raped, a charge she later withdrew.

That night, the mob broke into the jailhouse. Having taken away and murdered two of the men, the killers came back chanting 'We want Cameron. We want Cameron.' The boy was dragged out amid blows and curses. Around him he saw faces he knew — people whose lawns he'd mown and messages he'd run. He was brought to the place of execution. 'More fists, more clubs, more bricks and rocks found their mark,' he remembered. A noose was put around his neck. 'I waited for the end.'

At that point there was an intervention. A woman's voice rang out: 'Take the boy back. He had nothing to do with any raping and killing.'

A strange thing happened. Silence fell. Hands holding clubs and gasoline cans were lowered. The boy stood up, alone in a mob of 15,000, someone's hands removed the rope around his neck and a path opened in front of him as, limping and 'saying a prayer with every step', he made his way back to the jailhouse. The sheriff put him a car and drove him to safety in a town 50 kilometres away. Cameron was charged with accessory to robbery, served five years and was freed.

But who had called out? Whose voice — 'sharp and crisp like bells on a winter's day', Cameron said years later — saved him? He never knew. He grew up and became a civil rights activist, and is the only person known to have survived a lynching in the United States.

This odd story emerged in 1994 and came with no further explanation. I was interested because I knew the Billie Holiday song and Nina Simone's version and had often seen the photograph. I was working on a paper in London at the time and I asked one of our correspondents in the US to find Cameron and interview him, which he duly did. I ran his short report and the infamous photograph in the foreign pages of the paper.

I was almost more surprised by what happened next than by the story itself. The editor complained. He spoke up at the next editorial conference and said he disliked the story about the lynch mob. What was it for? What did it *mean*? Journalism existed to supply answers, not to set out new mysteries. It occurred to me later he may have been offended by a line that had emerged from the interview. Cameron, after thinking the matter over for years, had come to the conclusion that it was not a human but a supernatural agency which saved him. It was the voice, he speculated, of an angel, and he had been spared for a reason — to educate Americans about the horrors of lynching. The editor was a strict secularist and was probably irritated to see this angel put on the record, without derision, in his own newspaper.

I understood his objection. It would have been better if another explanation had been found — if the mysterious speaker had been located and interviewed. Was it the woman who alleged rape in the first place? She alone, after all, might have had enough authority to turn the mob back. *He had nothing to do with any raping.* But she was no more available for interview than the angel, and I still thought the story had merit, if only as a postscript to the photograph and Abel Meeropol's song. But I stood reprimanded.

I admired my editor — he was a man of swift and penetrating intelligence, he had done me several good turns, and he knew far more about the British reader and the British press than I ever would. If he said this story, which I particularly liked, was not good journalism then he would know. And therefore I should be off. I did leave the paper a year later, and in a way that was one of the reasons. The voice which made a mob fall silent one night in Marion, Indiana, also, by a series of remote connections, sent me out the door of a newspaper on the other side of the Atlantic over 60 years later and, by extension, then being free to follow other interests, driving out of Christchurch towards the mountains with Paddy McMahon to look for an eagle we knew wasn't there.

The mountains, meanwhile, were no longer in sight. The plains outside Christchurch are as flat as a billiard table but the table is on a slant and the peaks on the horizon seem to get lower as you approach; as well as that the windbreaks of pines and macrocarpa and blue-gums had grown much taller than I remembered and they blocked the views. Then the road veered slightly towards the west and suddenly there it was — the entire Torlesse Range filling the windscreen. But which of the peaks was Tāwera?

Charles Torlesse was a surveyor and the first European to climb any mountain in the Southern Alps, and both the peak he climbed and the whole range were named after him. Then confusion immediately crept in. Some of the Māori names as noted down by the British settlers were at variance with one another or wrongly transcribed, so that Whatarama, for instance, which may have been the original name for the whole range, became Otarama, which the settlers thought was the correct Māori name and Māori thought was a strange new English name. Meanwhile some of the English names — Trinity, Rubicon — were later replaced by other, generally more boring ones — Back Peak, Red Peak and so on.

And if that wasn't enough, one tribal tradition has it that the peak named Tāwera was not in the Torlesse Range at all but just across the river in the form of a high hill known as Mount Oxford or Oxford Hill (or, according to the sketchbook of Torlesse, then a young, unmarried man, Little Nipple, as distinct from Great Nipple further north). One expert, having thought about the matter for years, decided Tāwera had been the name of not one but two mountains, separate but side by side on the north and south banks of the Waimakariri River, which is possible but seems rather unlikely.[2]

As we drove over the plains, therefore, there was a kind of midge-dance of nomenclature over all the valleys and peaks in front of us, as indeed there had once been over the plains themselves which, between 1840 and 1850, were known variously as Ngā Pākihi-whakatekateka-a-Waitaha — The Open Plains where Waitaha Walked Proudly — the Port Cooper Plains, the Great Southern Plain, the Wilberforce Plain, the Sumner Plain and the Whateley Plain, before settling down as the Canterbury Plains, which so far they remain. The rivers which run across them, and the largest lake in the locality, were renamed after various English lords (Cholmondeley, Courtenay, Ashley, Ellesmere) living in castles on the other side of the world, but some of these new names failed to take and quite soon two of the biggest rivers, the Rakaia and the Waimakariri, sprawling in their mile-wide shingle beds, quietly resumed their Māori identity . . .

None of this, strictly speaking, mattered to us since the hunting range of the eagle was probably 50 square kilometres and any Pouākai nesting on 'a spur of Tawera' would have flown out and looked down on the whole assemblage of peaks and scree and tussock and braided rivers with a cool, property-owning eye. We came closer and closer to the range, then Paddy turned and we dived down a side road. A clump of pines with ruddy trunks, three unshorn rams in a ram paddock, a shuttered Christian youth camp, a rusty railway line curving out of sight . . . Paddy knew all these Canterbury nooks and crannies.

The road began to climb and we shot up a steep lane, parked and got out. There were houses and letterboxes on one side of the road — this was almost suburban and not at all what I was looking for — and we walked out on open land on the other side where the grass was long and dank in the shadow of a swag of pines which blocked the view. I was beginning to doubt the value of this excursion — then the pines gave way and suddenly there we were.

Eagle habitat.

Behind us rose the peaks where *Harpagornis* had nested. Below us, hazy plains stretched for 250 kilometres north to south. That was the Larder. Down there, giant moa had once roamed in such numbers that when settlers from Europe arrived they could not pull a plough through the earth in some places, it was so thickly sown with moa bones.

'Well, if *I* was an eagle . . .' I said, and we started kidding around in the excited lingo of real estate agents —

'Dress-circle residence!'

'Superb transport links!'

'Handy all amens!'

— but the same time a very different sense was coming over me: I had never seen it from this vantage point before but the whole landscape was intensely familiar — that rag of haze in the middle distance was Christchurch, and the mild humps behind it were the Port Hills where I roamed about as a boy. But now, mainly because the great eagle was in my mind, I saw the sheer grandeur of the place — the great rivers Waimakariri and Rakaia issuing from the wall of mountains and crossing the plains to the blue sea which that morning was indistinguishable from the sky — and I began to see that it was not a fluke, an error on the part of nature, that the greatest of the eagles had evolved right here and not in some more distinguished neighbourhood of the planet such as the Himalayas or the Andes.

I had read somewhere that the *orogeny* of the Southern Alps — the rate at which they are rising or being pushed into the sky — is one of the highest in the world, and that if this chain of mountains had happened to be in a quieter climatic zone then the tallest of them, Aoraki Mount Cook, would now stand at 52,000 feet or 15,850 metres, nearly twice the height of Everest, but the rate of *erosion* of these peaks standing on their island in the Roaring Forties (Tiritiri o te Moana — Mirage of the Ocean — is their Māori name) is also the highest in the world, the stream of westerly gales being almost endless and constantly battering them down, so that Aoraki Mount Cook is only a modest 3724 metres. And then *this* idea, of the rising and falling of mountains like the dance of hills and valleys in Isaiah, made it plain not only that the evolution of the eagle here was not a fluke, but that *Harpagornis* had been the most exact and vivid living representative of the land I could see around me.

And then, for the first time, I began to feel a kind of pride in the place, which I left when I was fourteen and hardly thought about since. I had claims here, I thought, not exactly of ownership but of belonging: all four of my grandparents and at least two great-grandparents and a whole host of great-aunts and great-uncles and cousins once or twice removed now lay buried down there in the haze between the two rivers. Walkers, Ravens, Knyvetts, MacDonalds.

Then I thought, *But I don't know where any of them are.*

I could not at that moment have gone and stood by the grave of a single one of them. Where was Great-grandma O'Rourke who would never leave the house locked in case some traveller needed shelter on a cold rainy night? Where were her five sons who went to the Western Front together and all came back, not a hair on the head of one of them harmed, and who then, according to family lore, sat on the veranda of the farmhouse at Levels quietly sipping whisky until the roar went out of their heads, and then one by one slipped away to resume their normal lives? Where was Charlie Knyvett who had 5000 acres — or was it 10,000? — on the north bank of the Rakaia, and who could not pull a plough through the earth for all the moa bones . . .

Where — and this really did me make me feel ashamed — was my favourite relative, my daredevil Aunt Roma who taught me to drive and then, scandalised that at the age of ten I had never 'done the ton' — gone a hundred miles an hour — got behind the wheel of the powder-blue Jag, the driver's door still battered after Wayfarer, the stallion at the farm in Prebbleton, escaped from his paddock and, chasing Roma through her own always unkempt rose garden, turned and kicked it with his hind hooves when she dived inside. Cigarette in hand, with me in the passenger seat, Roma now took off and, wavering at first, sped up and drove straight as an arrow on one of the long shingle roads that cross the plains — 80, 90, 100 — rushing towards the blue wall of mountains where Paddy and I were now standing.

I had no idea where Roma was buried.

This I felt was a serious charge against me, and I didn't like it. And it was not at all why I had come to Tāwera: I was quite pleased when Paddy said it was time to go. He had planned a full programme for the day. The view in front of us was just the opening panorama; now he wanted to walk into the heart of the range. If you're going on a wild goose chase, at least do it properly — that was Paddy's view.

We went back to the highway and drove about 15 kilometres, parked, went through a five-barred gate and began to walk up a wide stony valley. This was a very different landscape — hot, sheltered, treeless. The only sound was the occasional *tink* as a stone shifted in the little river, the Kōwai, which came stepping down neatly through the scrub, and the only sign of life was the air traffic around a few beehives stacked in faded pink boxes, like office blocks, in the mānuka.

These mountain valleys had looked very different in the pre-European period when Tāwera and the whole range was a famous hunting ground, richly forested, teeming with kiwi and kiore and kākāpō, the great green night-parrot which was prized for its sweet-smelling pelt, and also as a household pet where it occupied the niche now taken by the domestic cat. The kākāpō was hunted by Māori on moonlit nights with specially trained dogs. 'If the dog knows its job, well and good, but if it doesn't — the kakapo can kick like a horse, and ka kiki te waewae [if the leg kicks] it is a serious matter for a dog.'[3]

Now kākāpō, kiwi and forest had all vanished like the moonlight of another century and Paddy and I could have been walking up some bare valley in Crete or the Peloponnese — it was hard to believe, in any case, that Christchurch with its green parks and willowy rivers was only 40 minutes away.

Paddy thought that over-grazing and repeated burning off by farmers had probably done the damage although it was possible, he said, that this particular valley had always been dry and bare in the rain shadow. The further in we walked the hotter it got and the Kōwai got smaller as we passed its tributaries, but then we came to a place where the water pooled beside a rock and was just deep enough to swim in, so we jumped in and lay there looking at the crags high above us. Paddy had climbed all the peaks up there when he was young but we agreed there was no need for us go any further. There are probably dozens of pools and tarns around the base of the range which fit the legend of Tāwera, but the one we were in was as good as any:

> At length a brave man called Te Hau o Tawera came on a visit to the neighbourhood and finding that the people . . . were so paralysed with fear . . . he volunteered to capture and kill this rapacious bird, provided they would do what he told them. This they willingly promised, and having procured a quantity of manuka saplings he went one night with fifty men to the foot of the hill, where there was a shallow pool, sixty feet in diameter. This he completely covered over with a network formed of saplings, and under this he placed the fifty men armed with spears and thrusting weapons, while he himself as soon as it was light, went out to lure the Pouakai from its nest.
>
> He did not go far before that 'destroyer' spied him and swooped down upon him. Hautere [Te Hau] had now to run for his life and just succeeded in reaching the shelter of the network when the bird pounced on him, and in its violent efforts to reach its prey, forced its legs through the meshes, and becoming entangled, the fifty men plunged their spears into its body and after a desperate encounter succeeded in killing it.[4]

This valley we were in was also the route young Charles Torlesse took centuries later when he came to the mountain in 1849. He had arrived in the district a few days before with a party of British officials and surveyors looking for a site for

91

a new colony to be named Canterbury. Torlesse was born in Suffolk, near the Essex border, and probably had never seen a line of snowy peaks stretching north and south a hundred miles on a summer morning. 'How I would like to see what is on the other side of that,' he said, looking towards Tāwera, and the chief surveyor gave him permission to go. He set off from the base of the mountain at dawn on New Year's Day, with a Māori named George Tuwhia, a local boy as a guide, a donkey and 'a dog for company'. They reached the summit about four in the afternoon, 'not having rested or fed since starting'. Torlesse recorded that it was 'Warm on East side, Bitterly cold on the West, there being a strong wind from the snowy mountains. Drank deliciously cold snow water.'[5]

He had gone to see what was on the other side but it turned out there was no other side. All that could be seen were more mountains rising higher and higher in the west. He made a rapid sketch of peaks to the south and then the whole party — Tuwhia, Torlesse, boy, dog and donkey — turned and raced all the way down, following the Kōwai, and reached shelter about eight o'clock while it was still light. Torlesse then spent two weeks criss-crossing the plains, cutting through creeks and swamps, hunting wild dogs for sport and running the soil through his fingers.

On 10 January 1849, while camping on the south bank of the Waimakariri, he wrote in his diary: 'Had several Maories from the pah to breakfast. (Flash Charley whom Willis knocked down among the rest.) Lost my telescope. Some korero about the white man's land being South of the Coldstream [Waimakariri], and the Maories' North.'

He did not know it but just then Torlesse was brushed by

the wing of the legend of the Pouākai, and he was also playing a part in a great drama between the races which had begun a few months before and was to continue for a century and a half.

In January 1849 the situation in the South Island was this: about two years earlier the chiefs of the local tribe, Ngāi Tahu, decided to sell most of the plains to the colonial government. Their asking price was £5 million. Preposterous, said the British, who made a counter-offer of £2000. This might have been the point for bargaining to commence but there was an imbalance of power between the parties as vast as the gap between the sums of money. Ngāi Tahu was a small tribe, no more than 2000 people, much weakened by civil war and then invasion by another tribe, Ngāti Toa, from the North Island. Britain had an empire of hundreds of millions of people. A gunboat, aptly named the *Acheron*, was already sailing up and down the coast.

Threats were made. If Ngāi Tahu did not accept the British terms, the money would be given to Ngāti Toa, who had come and gone but still claimed ownership through right of conquest. The British admitted their offer to Ngāi Tahu was rather low but they promised *ample* — always the same word — reserves, traditional hunting grounds and fishing stations, while schools and hospitals would be built for the Māori of the south, who would then live side by side with their British brothers and sisters.

Ngāi Tahu wavered. Most of the chiefs wanted to accept the British offer, but on certain conditions. There were places they would not part with, for example the land on the north bank of the Waimakariri River. This was their heartland, the site of their fallen capital, Kaiapoi, the scene of their greatest battles, where the bones of the warriors who had died two decades earlier still lay unburied, too tapu to touch.

The Waimakariri block comprised about 260,000 acres of flat land and gently rolling country with the mountains in the background. Here is a description of the district in 1848 as imagined by a modern writer: 'Grassland, wetlands and forest, backed by bold mountain ranges capped with winter snow . . . The plains and downlands, ideal for farming, abounded with weka, koreke and wild pigs. There were fine plantations of cabbage trees. Three ancient podocarp forests, the largest remaining on the plains, held a wealth of bird-life and timber. Streams of crystal-clear water gushed from underground sources, nourishing a maze of channels, swamps and lagoon rich with eels, lampreys, waterfowl and fish . . . Kakapo and other choice birds inhabited the vast beech forests of Tawera . . .'[6]

The government agent agreed to this exemption, the deal was signed and the vendors went home to await payment. Three months later, people living on the north side of the river looked up and saw an extraordinary sight. There was a group of Europeans calling and gesticulating on the south bank of the river. One of the men was named Walter Mantell. He was the leader, a young official with an impressive government position — Commissioner for Extinguishing Native Title — and he was carrying an accordion. His second in command, a Mr Wills, was a surveyor and was carrying a theodolite. A shouted conversation took place across the water. *Who* were they? What did they want again?

They had come, said Mantell, to establish a reserve for Māori use. There was no need, said Ngāi Tahu — it was all reserved for their use. Very well, said Mantell, I need to establish the northern boundary of the block. The arguments continued for some hours. Mantell is the main source of information, but his diary, his sketchbook and his official report are at variance with one another and in any case not very clear. It seems that it was not until the next day that he was allowed over the river.[7]

Clever and ambitious, Mantell had previously worked as a postmaster in Wellington and then as an overseer of a gang of Māori road workers. As postmaster he managed to make himself hated in the little capital. Letters were written to the papers complaining about him. He was lazy. He was a liar. He was cruel. If a ship was sailing for England that night, Mantell would close the post office early so that people running down the hill to send a letter home would be disappointed.

While working with the road gang he learned to speak Māori; he then seems to have been stood down, or he took leave, and went to Taranaki, where he stole a large cache of fossils, of moa and other birds, to ship off to England. There can be no doubt about the theft: decades later Mantell made an airy apology to the rightful owner, who had found the deposits, for the 'grievous poaching which I committed on his manor'.[8]

He was in New Plymouth, waiting to ship the fossils off to his father in England, when Governor Grey arrived in town, heard of the treasures and came to see them.

Something about Mantell — perhaps his defects — appealed to the governor. Not long afterwards, and quite unexpectedly, he appointed him to the role of Extinguisher of Title, with almost plenipotentiary powers to decide the size of the reserves which the Māori in the South Island would be left to live on.

Even without his official title, he was well named for the task. 'Mantell' derives from the verb 'to mantle' — to cover, conceal, darken, hide a fault. Once across the river, the Extinguisher hid his real intentions for three days. Then on Saturday morning, 2 September 1849, he made his move. His diary suddenly takes an imperious tone: 'I told' — but this is crossed out, and he starts again — 'I set out with them for the sand hills to show them what I would consent to give them . . . Arrived at the sand hills I led them on . . . and pointed out the limits of the reserve.'

It was there, standing on a dune in mid-morning, the sun high in the sky and the boom of surf sounding from the beach, that Mantell revealed the scale of the injustice about to strike Ngāi Tahu. Of the 260,000 acres of the Waimakariri block, he would *consent to give them* 2600 acres. Nor was that the end of it. The land now to be taken by the British did not stop, as the sellers had intended, at the foothills along the edge of the plains. All the mountains beyond, as far as the other coast, Mantell now declared to be British property as well.

What happened next is also not very clear. 'A great consultation followed,' Mantell's diary states. As might well be expected: for an outlay of £2000 the British Empire, here taking the form of Walter Mantell, claimed ownership of 20 million acres, at 10,000 acres a pound, or 40 acres a penny, or 10 acres a farthing — land that would soon be on sale to settlers at £3 an acre. The Māori owners, meanwhile, who when they woke that morning would not have been able to point out the boundaries of their property which lay beyond the horizon, were now, in effect, paupers.

Then, according to Mantell, all opposition vanished. The Māori suddenly agreed 'to the limits as I described them', he reported to Lieutenant-Governor Eyre, who was now overseeing the transaction. Great scepticism is called for here. Eyre had already made it clear that he had no objection if Māori kept the Waimakariri block. The decision to strip them of their heartland was Mantell's own, and it was in his interests to make it seem a harmless and unexceptionable act: a *consultation* . . . followed by *agreement.*

'I called several times on any dissentient and none appearing requested Mr Wills to commence the survey,' Mantell wrote.

The 'dissentients' had evidently gone away en masse. Silence fell over the sandhills.

The silence lasted another day: 'Sunday: In camp' is all Mantell's journal has to say. On Monday things began to heat up. 'Two or three old men, not understanding the erection of a [survey] pole at their huts at Waitueri, threw it away. I went down lectured them explained use of pole and remained there. Very excited speeches all night.'

The next day came the explosion. The young Māori known to the British as 'Flash Charley' arrived on the scene. His real name was — well, what *was* his real name? Like certain mountains and rivers, some Māori in the nineteenth century existed in a kind of haze of names. At birth, the young chief had been named after his father, Pakipaki, which means 'Applause', and he used this intermittently for the rest of his days. As a youth, however, he also took an English name,

George Williams, which he usually rendered as Teoti Wiremu. Then later, probably in his mid-twenties when he was working on an American whaling ship or just after he came home, he took a new Māori name, Te Hau, and its cognate, Metehau, which means '*like* Te Hau'.

Hau is a potent word in Māori with a wide range of meanings — breath, wind, dew, brisk, fresh, cool, illustrious, commanding — and it has been suggested that young Pakipaki/George Williams/Teoti Wiremu took the name Te Hau ('the wind') or Metehau ('like the wind') as a kind of memorandum of the time he spent before the mast on the American sailing ship.[9] This is possible but it seems far more likely that he was thinking of Te Hau o Tāwera, the hero who killed the Pouākai on the mountain named Tāwera. He must have known the story well, for Metehau was an owner of the mountain where the legend was set.

Māori ownership rights were more complex than the British believed. There was a famous incident in the previous century, probably about 1740, when Ngāi Tahu chiefs were portioning out the territory for their own use.

'As they approached the mountain known as Whatarama, they each claimed a peak of the range. "That is mine," cried Tane-tika, "that the kakapo skins may form a kilt for my daughter, Hine-mihi."

'"That is mine," cried Hika-tutae, "that the kakapo skins may form a girdle for my daughter, Kai-ata."

'Moki had his servant with him who whispered in his ear. "Wait, do not claim anything yet."

'And then the man climbed a tree.

'"What are you doing there?" said the rest of the party.

'"Only breaking off the dry branches to light our fires with."

'But in reality he was looking out for the mountain . . . where kakapo were most abundant. Presently he espied the far-famed peak.

'"My mountain is Kura-tawhiti," he cried.

'"Ours!" said Moki.

'The claim was at once recognised by the others and Moki's descendants have ever since enjoyed the exclusive right to hunt kakapo on Kura-tawhiti.'[10]

Since Metehau claimed land on Kura-tawhiti, it is likely he was a descendant of the celebrated Moki, and since he claimed eight pieces of land on neighbouring Tāwera, either through Moki or another ancestor, we can sense a powerful resonance in his new name. Coming back to New Zealand in about 1841 after his years abroad — possibly it was from his American shipmates that he acquired his mistrust of British motives — he found the British already in charge and Māori land being alienated at an accelerating rate. Did he take the name Te Hau, or Metehau, because he believed there was a dangerous new predator — a huge, land-hungry empire — on the wing, that 'none could escape its talons', and that it was up to him to find a way to defeat it?

It was about this time that he also acquired the name 'Flash Charley' among the settlers. It was not a term of endearment. Worldly, untrusting, literate, possibly a dandy (although in the early nineteenth century 'flash' also had the connotation of 'not easily fooled'),[11] he was exactly the sort of man colonial officials detested. While in the North Island, Metehau had been a close observer in the law courts and in the field of skirmishes already taking place between

Māori and settlers over land. At one point he was taken on as crew on the governor's own ship, but was then put ashore on suspicion of being a spy. When he heard that part of his own homeland was going up for sale, he hurried back to the South Island and was among the few who absolutely opposed the transaction. But he was young and had few supporters. The deal went ahead.

When Mantell arrived in the Waimakariri block, Metehau's darkest premonitions must have seemed to be coming true. He is mentioned scornfully in the diary notes Mantell made on the first day ('Metehau is great in the knowledge of the true value of the land') but then he seems to disappear. It was only on the Tuesday that he comes back into view. Evidently he had just learned that his own property, the two mountains Tāwera and Kura-tawhiti, were being claimed by the Extinguisher.

He rushed out to stop the surveying party. There was an altercation and the survey stopped. Metehau then ran to the surveyors' camp and set fire to Wills' hut. Wills came after him and the two men fought. Wills knocked his opponent down, or later told people he did, and if he did then Metehau got up and started to tear down Mantell's tent. Mantell arrived and Metehau snatched up an axe or mere, or perhaps a large adze — a toki is mentioned in some accounts — and ran at Mantell, who took out his gun and primed it and then, amidst the smoke and shouting, some Christian chiefs came up and held the young firebrand back.

Their line was as follows: this must all be a terrible mistake. A Christian queen such as Victoria would never allow a man of low degree like Mantell to commit obvious fraud in her name.

Metehau did not share this optimism but allowed himself

to be restrained. Mantell retreated to his tent and heard more 'excited speeches' which lasted all night. He understood Māori quite well and, listening through the canvas, he concluded he had lost the battle for the Waimakariri block and might as well pack up and go back over the river in the morning. There the story might have ended, but there are times destiny or the stars prefer an extended narrative. 'The only reason for time is so that everything doesn't happen at once.'[12] This story needed a century or more to reveal its meaning.

When Mantell stepped out of his tent in the morning, he found everyone looking at the horizon to the south. Smoke could be seen 50 kilometres away on Banks Peninsula. A ship was about to sail to Wellington. Almost all the chiefs then set out on foot to catch the ship and complain to the governor in person about Mantell. This suited the Extinguisher of Title perfectly — he was left to finish laying out the tiny reserve for Māori in the Waimakariri block, and then he went back across the river to carry on southward over the plains to complete his task of extinguishing elsewhere.

This was roughly the situation when young Charles Torlesse arrived in the district a few months later and had 'several Maories from the pah to breakfast', Metehau among them, on the bank of the river.

Metehau was the only man who physically took a stand against Mantell, but after that the Extinguisher had vanished like a bad dream — perhaps nothing would come of his visit. The young chief must have been alarmed a few months later when another Englishman was seen roaming the plains, and even climbing about on Tāwera. Metehau went to see Torlesse and make matters plain: *The white man's land was south of the river, Māori land to the north.*

Did Metehau take Torlesse's telescope that morning? We have no way of knowing, although it must have crossed Torlesse's mind when he offered his visitors a reward for finding it. Were the British planning to steal his mountains? Metehau could not be sure. Not long after Torlesse's visit, he sat down to write a letter. The fact that he had pen, ink, paper and sealing wax to hand in that wild land speaks to a presence of mind equal to his confidence. His letter (here translated) was to the Queen of England:

'April 2, 1849

'Speed this my friendly address to London, to Queen Victoria.

'Madam — O, Queen — Tena Koe. There you are. Greetings. Great is my regard for you.

'Madam, let your clemency be shown to us, as our respect for you is great, even unto the end. Even to you also because you have become as near as a relation can be to us, because New Zealand has been named as a messenger of wealth to the Queen.

'Friend, Victoria, greetings to you who now live in your country. My address to you is this. With regard to my pieces of land — I have retained them because I was not one of the parties who consented to sell the land. I have retained them for my permanent use. They are not large pieces, they are small. Had I consented to sell the land, I should not have retained these pieces. Those who consented to sell have their own way of thinking about the matter. These pieces we are now claiming are not large pieces, they are small. Let your clemency therefore be shown to us, and to New Zealand generally, because these lands are our own and were handed down to us by our Ancestors. The pieces my Father had is the portion I now claim. The portion of Te Kuratawhiti and Te Tawera. There is [also] the pa of Kaiapoi. These are small pieces but the number of acres will tell.

'These are the portions of land I wish to retain. This is my friendly address to you, and therefore be kind to us.

'Madam, Victoria, send a reply to this letter.'[13]

Madam never replied. This was perhaps not her fault. Metehau's letter was opened in Wellington and sent to Governor Grey in Auckland. He asked for information about Metehau but, like a man enquiring into his own adultery, he was not in search of the facts. He was delighted with his new policy in the South Island — millions of acres had fallen into his hands for a few pounds, while the reserves set aside for Māori were as small as possible.

Grey turned to Mantell and Wills for information about the writer. They were pleased to provide bad notices. Metehau was a 'cunning troublesome fellow' said Wills, 'all too familiar with native successes' in early quarrels over land in the North Island. Mantell's reply was extraordinary. Four pages of vituperation were not too many to vent his ill-feeling: 'I have known the native in question since 1841 . . . Even at that time he bore a bad character. Since then he has been leading a vagabond life . . . The prospect of gain induced him, on hearing of the sale of his native district, to return thither. He had before then acquired the name "Flash Charley" . . . At Te Tuahiwi he assaulted Mr. Wills, set fire to a hut erected by our men and was forcibly held back by the other natives while seeking to attack me with a tomahawk . . . He is respectably descended but by no means a chief.

His influence if he can acquire any can only spring from his success in opposition to the government. Finding himself a stranger in his own country, he brings with him all the low cunning and imperfect knowledge of our customs which he has acquired in his disreputable wanderings. He seeks with these to raise himself a party by which he may imitate those chiefs of this [North] Island of whom he is always speaking and whom he would so much wish to emulate, Rangihaeta [sic] and Heke. Since his misconduct at Tuahiwi I have declined to hold any association with him.'[14]

This satisfied the governor: Metehau could be safely ignored. There is no sign the letter in translation was sent on to London, and the original remains in the files in Wellington, sealing wax still bright red above the name and address of the Queen of England.

Yet there was still a chance, when Torlesse and Metehau met by the river in January 1849, that things might turn out well. Torlesse's diary suggests an even-tempered encounter. 'Some korero about the white man's land south of the river.'

Kōrero is a moderate term: talk, discussion, discourse. Torlesse himself, though obnoxious at times ('I killed a horse and a maori the other day,' he wrote to his mother back in England, 'that is to say, they died of some cause or another') was sympathetic to the Māori claim to the land on the north bank. He disapproved of Mantell, of the sale proceedings in general, the miserable payment and the woefully small reserves.

'The Maories have just received . . . payment for the country,' he told his mother, 'but the purchase has been effected, I am afraid, in such a loose manner, and the amount of money has been so small . . . the recipients have named His Excellency "Governor Hiccapenny" [Governor Sixpence] in consequence. Besides . . . the natives deny the sale of some of the land which by [Mantell's] account is duly purchased. But Mantell is a notoriously indolent man, and naturally incapable . . . of conducting a business which requires remarkable forbearance and caution. Because they are few in number, the natives are to be neglected, a circumstance not much to the credit of the government.'[15]

Mantell had now left the stage; there was reason to hope someone better might arrive. And a very strange entity, unlike any seen in any other British colony of the nineteenth century, was about to appear on the plains. Here, in order of precedence, are the members of the Canterbury Association, set up in London in 1847 to establish a new settlement in the South Pacific: the Archbishop of Canterbury, the Archbishop of Dublin, the Duke of Buccleugh, the Marquis of Cholmondeley, the Earl of Ellesmere, the Earl of Harewood, the Earl of Lincoln MP, Viscount Mandeville MP, the Bishop of London, the Bishop of Winchester, the Bishop of Exeter, the Bishop of Ripon, the Bishop of St David's, the Bishop of Oxford, the Bishop of Norwich, Viscount Alford MP, Lord Ashburton, Lord Lyttelton, Lord Ashley MP, Lord Courtenay, Lord Alfred Hervey MP, Lord John Manners — plus a swarm of baronets and knights and younger sons, Custs and Cavendishes and other great families.

The new Canterbury was described as the 'most aristocratic colony since Virginia'. Few Liberals or Whigs were on the list. The members of the Canterbury Association were almost all high church and Tory, apart from Lord Ashley, later the Earl of Shaftesbury, who was a low-church evangelical but who famously saved the infant chimney sweeps of England, and the 'lunatics', from their cruel mistreatment. He was allowed to join the association on account of his philanthropy.

Philanthropy in a way was at the heart of the project, as it was not for the aristocratic Virginians. Their lordships, spiritual and temporal, who formed the association of 1847 were aghast at the England which had sprung up in the last few decades — a nightmare land of satanic mills and sunless slums where the poor had lost contact with their past, the countryside, their religion and their betters. The great Whig families, in alliance with a ruthless new class of capitalists, had destroyed the bonds which once held the people together.

Instead of reforming England, however, the Canterbury Association had another idea. Far away in a fairyland in the South Pacific a new England could be built, or rather an old England rebuilt, where rich and poor, titled and commoners, would live together, or at least meet at the lych-gate, bound together by respect for rank and a sense of duty, not least the duties of the rich to the poor.

The source of this vision, John Robert Godley, was the nephew of an Irish peer, Lord Dunsandle. Tall, spare, with a high, domed forehead and wide-set, pale eyes, Godley was fascinated by the responsibility of power. During the Irish famine it was said that not one of the Dunsandle tenants died of hunger, at least when he was in charge. This was more unusual than it might sound. Godley was particularly interested in methods of colonising. The Greeks, he wrote, had learned to 'transport a perfect type of the parent society . . . the art . . . has, apparently, not descended to us.'[16] Everywhere he looked, the infant colonies or former (American) colonies of Britain were caricatures of the parent.

Race relations were an obvious problem. In 1842 Godley travelled to North America. He was a natural conservative, and a paternalist, almost prepared to believe the pro-slavery argument that slaves were better off, better fed and clothed, more *contented* than freedmen. What he found outraged him. 'I came away more impressed with the convictions of the evils of slavery than when I entered the slave states,' he wrote.

Hatred was at the heart of the matter — the 'mingled contempt and abhorrence which the white feels for the black, whom he can hardly bring himself to regard as a human being'.

Even in Virginia (he didn't reach the Deep South) he noted the slaves' 'miserable appearance . . . two or more families living in one hut, and that of the worst, and the children generally naked . . . It is absolutely forbidden by law to teach them to read or write. No religious lessons were allowed.' To prevent the education of *immortal beings* — that, Godley wrote, was 'absolutely and *per se* criminal . . . I should deem hardly any sacrifice too great, short of actual civil war . . .

to get rid of slavery which I believe to be . . . a crying and grievous evil.'[17]

Seven years later Godley was in a position to put his own theories to the test, on what seemed to be a blank canvas on the other side of the world. After spending about three weeks in the South Island, Charles Torlesse's boss, Chief Surveyor Captain Thomas, decided that the plains were the place for Godley's 'Canterbury'. Things then moved with incredible speed, unimaginable today. The news was sent to London, a new port of Lyttelton, the town of Christchurch and a road between them were surveyed, thousands of colonists and emigrants (colonists were rich; emigrants poor) gathered on the wharves of England, and Godley and his wife Charlotte put to sea a few months ahead of them.

The Godleys came ashore in New Zealand late in 1849 and took up residence in Canterbury in 1850. Their first stop after disembarkation was Christchurch, which was still a waste of tussock and swamp. There was another peculiarity to Godley's dream vision. Canterbury was not only to be a simulacrum of England, old England as seen below a rainbow, with all its ranks and orders, it was more particular still: it was to be a kind of replica of an Oxford college, and not just any college but *his* old college, namely Christ Church, the wealthiest and most snobbish of all the colleges — so superior to the others, in fact, that the word 'college' was never added to the name, although it was (and is) sometimes called 'House'.

At the centre of Christ Church, Oxford, was the chapel, also called Christ Church, which served as the cathedral for the town itself. Very well — at the heart of the new antipodean Christchurch (one word) would stand a great cathedral,

ChristChurch (two words, no gap), with the quadrangles of university and grammar school nearby.

By the time Godley arrived, Captain Thomas had prepared the plan for this town, although it was not quite finished — the botanic gardens were still floating about and the university college was also in motion, shifting further away from the cathedral for more space, but everything else had been decided and it was not to be long before the first pinnacles of Victorian gothic began to rise in the swamp.

But what about the empty plains, the shining mountains beyond the town? How could they comport with Godley's vision? After leaving Christchurch — not a hut was built yet — the Godleys rode out across the empty plains. There were nine or ten in the party, including Godley's wife, Charlotte, their three-year-old son, Arthur, two leading settlers — Jerningham Wakefield and Frederick Weld — and Charles Torlesse as guide.

The first place he took them was the south bank of the Waimakariri. Torlesse adored the Godleys. 'Mr Godley is a thorough gentleman,' he wrote to his mother. 'I place great dependence on his generally correct management of this important and difficult business from his thoroughly high principles, great ability and sense of justice. Mrs Godley is the *beau ideal* of a lady. Waiting upon them was a real pleasure, I have not had such a treat since I left England.'[18]

Perhaps he had communicated some of his optimism to Ngāi Tahu. In any case optimism seemed to be in the air when the English party met Māori on the riverbank. Charlotte Godley wrote to her mother (many people in this story write home to their mothers — even the leading settlers were comparatively young) to describe the occasion. Both Torlesse and Wakefield also kept diaries, so we have a pretty good idea of what happened.[19]

Charlotte Godley: 'As it got a little dark, a party of natives . . . came over in a canoe to pay us a visit, and sit down by our fire . . . 'till we were all asleep in the tent we heard them singing and laughing.'

Torlesse: '. . . camped on the [river] the natives bringing in firewood and eels. Drank plenty of tea and sang songs till 11 p.m. and had a snug night of it.'

Wakefield: 'Camped drizzly weather from NE. Natives crossed over to us. Dissatisfied with bargain for land made with them by the Government. They caught plenty of delicate-flavoured eels for us.'

The next morning the English party crossed the river.

Torlesse: 'NE & NW. Very fine. Swam all the horses across the two branches of the river with Tinui's canoe. Natives all dressed out for the reception of the Governor as they call Mr. Godley.'

Wakefield: 'Swam the nine horses over both branches. Weld sent a native back for his shoes, promising him ten shillings to bring them to him by 12 the next day.

Charlotte Godley: '[The] natives . . . were expecting us to come and feast with them . . . and a very pretty place it was; but, as a feast *with* natives, it was rather a failure. For they gave us some *infantine* potatoes, much too young to eat, and some capital little fish, just like whitebait, from the river; and then sat round and looked at us, and smoked . . . It was pleasant sitting in shade, though, for the sun was really very hot that day.'

Wakefield: 'Here we camped two or three hours. I had a korero with the natives . . . Some dissatisfied ones have been clearing potato gardens in that part of the bush allotted to the Association. Godley inspected it. I warned the natives to proceed no further and to come in and discuss with the Governor-in-Chief, when he shall arrive, what has been done . . . We had very good whitebait, the hinanga in a younger state. Pink poppies wild here.'

A few hours later the Godleys rode across the block and stopped near the northern boundary, the Rakahuri (soon to be the Ashley) River.

Torlesse: 'At 2 p.m. whole party proceeded to Rangiora bush. Comfortably camped at Rangiora.'

Wakefield: 'We all slept outside our tent on account of the [sketch of a mosquito].'

Charlotte Godley: '. . . you must just imagine us there, just on the edge of thick, almost impenetrable wood, with very fine trees; and our little tent, with a fire at the door, quite shaded over by the tall waving toi-toi grass, and the large one for the gentlemen a little beyond, with such a magnificent fire. Mr. Weld, often as he had camped ... quite exclaimed in admiration at it ... He even went and got me a bouquet, that I wish I could send home for some of you to take to a ball! It was the flower of the cabbage tree, in size like an aloe, with a bunch of small whitish flowers, perhaps eighteen inches high, and sweet like hyacinths growing straight up out of the green leaves. We all sat round till the stars shone out, oh, so bright, and the owls began to hoot in the wood. It was a most lovely evening.'

One of the party, Frederick Weld, took out his watercolours. *A most lovely evening ...* The flower-head of the cabbage tree is on the tent pole. Arthur, three, has his mother's attention.

Someone is reading a map. Weld can't draw legs — it was a common Victorian failing; odd tubular limbs often appear in nineteenth-century sketches. Someone else, possibly Torlesse, is on his hands and knees in the grass. According to his dairies he was always losing things — his hat, his compass. For months he kept looking for his telescope even in places he had never been before. The fire is bright and the trees, dabbled with darkness, seem to be leaning in and the owls have begun to call — *ruru* in Māori, *morepork* in English.

It was, in fact, a crucial moment in the country's story. For a few hours everything hung in the balance. The Māori were right to call Godley 'Governor' — although he was not the governor of New Zealand as a whole, he was the only man in the country with enough authority, moral and social — all those archbishops and dukes at his back — to stand up to the actual governor and redress an arrangement which was patently unjust. By his own description, Godley was 'a perfect despot' in Canterbury, deciding the smallest matters. He must by then have known all the details of the land purchase by which the British, for an outlay of £2000, claimed ownership of 20 million acres.

And he knew by that night that the Māori disputed the sale of the Waimakariri block. He had seen people the same day clearing gardens with no thought of giving up their property. He did not need to be trained at law (though he was called to the bar in Dublin in 1831) to know the principle that property held in common cannot be sold without the consent of all the owners.

He must have known by heart the famous words of the founding treaty of the country which the British government had never abrogated: 'Her Majesty the Queen of England confirms and guarantees to the Chiefs and Tribes of New Zealand . . . the full exclusive and undisturbed possession of their Lands and Estates, Forests and Fisheries . . . so long as it is their wish and desire to retain the same in their possession.' He must have also known the *Instructions* of the Colonial Secretary, Lord Normanby, in 1839: 'The aborigines . . . must not be permitted to enter any contracts in which they might be the ignorant and unintentional authors of injuries to themselves. You will not, for example, purchase from them any territory the retention of which would be highly conducive to their own comfort, safety or subsistence.'

On the other hand, there were finances to consider. The Canterbury Association was badly in debt. The government had bought the land at about 500 acres a shilling but sold to the Association at 10 shillings an acre, and then roads and jetties and barracks and churches and offices had to be built. Land was to be sold on to settlers at £3 an acre, but sales had been slow. What would Godley do? What should he do? What would be the outcome of this night? The hour was late. Māori and Pākehā fell asleep in the forest, the trees leaning closer, the owls calling . . . *Ruru . . . Her Majesty confirms . . . ruru . . . undisturbed possession . . . morepork . . . 10 shillings an acre . . . morepork . . . 10 acres a farthing . . .*

The next day dawned fine. The party woke, breakfasted, packed up and left. Godley gave no sign of his thinking. They rode on and then split up, Weld going north, while the Godleys, Wakefield and Torlesse went west over the plains. After a few hours they stopped to survey their surroundings.

Charlotte Godley: 'Our next day's ride, about twenty long miles, took us to . . . a very pretty place, from the beauty of the woods, which are very extensive, and run over the hills, leaving patches of grass, so as to look just like fine park scenery.'

Wakefield: 'The scenery here is most beautiful. The gorges of the Ashley and some of its tributaries combine wood and cliff and water in great variety.'

Charlotte Godley: 'A good sized river comes through a deep-wooded rent in the rocks, two or three miles from the place we were at, and another small one only a quarter of a mile from us, across the plain.'

Wakefield: 'Oxford Hill straight above the forest, and Mounts Torlesse and Hutt to the south form a grand frame for the soft, park-like beauty of the edge of the forest.'

Charlotte Godley: 'We settled that those Colonists who aspire to a fine place, will locate themselves somewhere, there, where there are such magnificent situations.'

So there it was: *We settled that . . .*

The riders were still well inside the Waimakariri block and there, in sight of Mount Tāwera and the river named Ashley after the man who saved the child chimney sweeps, it was *settled* — Māori rights were to be ignored. These particular 'magnificent situations' were required by colonists, the gentry 'who aspire to a fine place'. It was probably foolish to have imagined any other outcome. It is generally accepted that the new province was called 'Canterbury' after the archbishop and primate of England, but the name had another, and probably a deeper, association for Godley, dating back to his student days which he never forgot.

His old college, Christ Church, was considered the grandest of all the Oxford colleges. Inside the gates, naturally, more hierarchies were to be found. There are three quadrangles in Christ Church: Great Quad or Tom's, Peckwater or Peck, and Canterbury. Canterbury is the smallest and was always the most exclusive. It was built in 1774, a small neo-classical square with splendid apartments for young men of noble birth and wealth. Godley was perhaps not one of them (Christ Church has not kept room records) but he knew and admired them and kept up with them all his life. This new Canterbury he planned on the other side of the world was perhaps, in his mind, not just to be a replica of his old college but a replica on a strange, vast scale, set about with snowy mountains, its cold rushing rivers named after lordly undergraduates — Cholmondeley, Courtenay, Ashley — who used to clatter up and down the stairs, of the most exclusive quadrangle in the oldest university in England.

Against this imperative, other considerations came second. Māori rights, for instance, could not be accommodated. The Māori of the Waimakariri block were allowed to keep five to ten acres each of their heartland. The rest of the land was divided between eleven wealthy colonists. Torlesse set aside his qualms and scrambled into an estate of 30,000 acres, and built his house at Rangiora, not far from the spot where the owls once called on a 'most lovely evening'.

He became a pillar of the local establishment and a justice of the peace — he was on the bench at the inquest into the death of the swagman Davis and 'sternly repressed' the indignation in the public gallery at the behaviour of George Moore. Later he succumbed to a personality disorder characterised by outbursts of rage and aggressive litigation against others, and he died comparatively young.

Metehau, owner of shadowy Tāwera, rich in forest and legend, seems not even to have got the standard allotment of five to ten acres. Perhaps he was penalised as a troublemaker. The *Lyttelton Times* in 1852 reported him living with his brother on 20 square feet of land — 'all that he could call his own' — the former site of his father's house which had been 'carved on all sides from the top to the bottom, carved all over', as befitted the dwelling of a chief.

North Island Māori must have known what happened in the south, and since it was now evident that promises the British made during sale negotiations were not to be relied on, many northern chiefs decided to sell no more land. Within a decade, war over this very matter broke out 'like a fire in the fern', as one chief famously put it, and soon the smoke filled all parts of the island.

Chapter 8

The Canterbury story, however, did not finish there. Even the personal duel between Mantell and Metehau was not over. They came face to face once again in 1879, almost exactly 30 years later, and very close to the place where the young chief had rushed at the Extinguisher with an axe. By 1879 everything looked completely different, as if a frantic set-designer had been at work. Gone were the cabbage tree groves, the carved houses, the laddered food-platforms and the illimitable horizons of the Māori world. In their place — a butcher, a baker, four churches, a bank built of bricks on one side of the main street and a post office clock tower of stone on the other. English willows and poplars rose above the chimney pots.

This was the new European town of Kaiapoi, a few miles from the ancient fortress of Kaiapoi and the new Māori settlement of Tuahiwi. Māori and Pākehā worlds, however, were closely connected. For three weeks in 1879, for example, hearings of a Royal Commission into Māori grievances over land were held in the European town. The Christchurch papers reported the proceedings: 'The large number of Natives assembled at Kaiapoi for the sitting of the Native Lands Commission are exceptionally well conducted . . . They leave the pah, which is two miles from town, in a coach-and-four and other vehicles in time to reach town for the sitting . . . Immediately the Commissioners take their seats, the utmost quiet and decorum is observed in the room among the two hundred or so who are usually present . . . many come with their notebooks and carefully jot down prominent portions of the evidence which form themes for discussion on the return to the pah in the evening.'[20]

On the third day of the hearing, Walter Mantell took the stand. He admitted that he knew in 1848 that Māori had requested their reserve stretch right across the island to the West Coast, and that he had the authority to grant the request, but 'I endeavoured to induce the Natives to accept as little as was possible'. He had drawn the reserves at Kaiapoi particularly closely, he said. 'Indeed I nearly had to shoot one gentleman about it, but then I was justified as he was on the point of tomahawking me. (Laughter.)'[21]

'When Mr Mantell said he was nearly tomahawked by a tattooed savage,' one reporter added, 'a highly respectable-looking elderly Native gentleman, sitting close to me, smiled grimly and whispered to me in excellent English: 'I'm d--- sorry now I didn't do it.'

This was Metehau. Thirty years on, Flash Charley had not lost his fire. Yet he must also have realised, long before, that running at Mantell with an axe, though a pleasing act of defiance, was not the way to defeat a rapacious empire at the height of its power. Slow, patient, more subtle tactics would be needed to outwit this predator. Strangely enough, it was Metehau, remembered today for the one thing that would never work — violent frontal assault — who also provided the method that would. *He wrote everything down.*

He wrote, as we saw, to the Queen of England, and following the affray with Mantell he wrote to him twice, and to Lieutenant-Governor Eyre, carefully listing all his landed property. Two years before Mantell had even set foot in the South Island, Metehau made an ōhākī, a statement which listed his personal holdings. Usually an ōhākī was made orally, on the deathbed of a chief, but Metehau made his as a young man, in good health, and in writing.[22]

He wrote as well to the newspapers on other matters — on the death of his wife, for instance, and on his family history, the tone always exquisitely courteous (*Ehoa ma e nga Pakeha katoa* — *My friends, all ye white people!*) and the fact that none of these letters had any effect at the time is beside the point. Metehau's letters and his ōhākī were not evocations of principle. They were not principally intended to stir the conscience of the reader. Their main purpose was to state and state again, in writing, to queen, governor, Mantell, anyone at all, who he was and what his property consisted of. *Eight pieces on Tawera. One piece on Kuratawhiti . . .*

Somewhere in his youthful wanderings he had come to the realisation that the great hungry empire had a weakness. The British were legally minded. They cared about the law, or at least the forms of law. They were particularly concerned about property and the rights of ownership. They also cared about paperwork. In 1848, when the Ngāi Tahu chiefs agreed to the Canterbury sale, most of them could not read or write, they made no maps themselves, and they put their faith in the honour of the buyer. 'We believed the white chief who bought the land: we said if this man does not keep his promise we will consider him a person of low degree.'

This statement was made 'in tones of mingled anger and contempt',[23] according to a reporter at the Kaiapoi hearing, by a chief who had signed the deed of sale 30 years before. What the vendors hadn't realised was that the government agent who arranged the deal couldn't care less at what degree they considered him.

Metehau, however, having seen the courts at work in the North Island, knew that the written word had stubborn, unchanging value. By 1879 most of the tribe had adopted Metehau's method: capture the fleeting word, write it down, repeat. *Many come with their notebooks and carefully jot down prominent portions of the evidence which form themes for discussion . . . in the evening . . .*

The reporters from Christchurch made several attempts to get into the night meetings at the pā, but 'the door was closed against us, as though it were barred and locked'. One night two of them more or less forced their way in. The overall impression they gained was of darkness and mystery. This was mid-autumn, the nights were getting cold, there were only one or two candles lit, the windows were closed and the air was thick. 'You could cut it and sell by the pound in Christchurch,' one of the press men wrote: 'From the entrance . . . doorway there poured no flood of light. What hazy, weird modification of darkness there was inside the building was . . . too feeble to struggle even a few inches into the outer blackness . . . My sight did not penetrate at any time more than half way up the hall; for all we could see, it might have stretched away to boundless space and been crowded by countless Maoris . . .'[24]

This was not at the old citadel of Kaiapoi that had fallen to the invaders from the north in the 1830s, and was never rebuilt. Ngāi Tahu did not go back. 'We were afraid of the sacred places,' a chief told the hearing in 1879. 'We were afraid of the blood of those who had been killed there, and their ghosts. We were afraid of the Maori deities.'[25] Instead, they built a new settlement, Tioriori (which means 'resounding' and probably refers to the sound of the sea) by the sandhills. Missionaries from England arrived in the district in the 1850s and one of them, John Raven, carefully gathered up and buried the bones of the fallen warriors which had been lying in sun and rain for a generation, while his colleague, John Stack, built a church at Tuahiwi, and so the people left the sandhills and went back inland.

Here we see the predicament of Ngāi Tahu. Their old terrors had gone. Fear of the old deities and of the blood and the ghosts of the fallen had receded, as had the threat of war. The wheatfields and flocks of sheep and the post office clock on the horizon signalled various things, but meant as well that no more Ngāti Toa war parties would ever come creeping up from the beach or down through the northern valleys. Ngāi Tahu had been saved from that for good.

But the threat had been replaced by another. The newcomers from Britain did not want to kill or enslave them, yet what they did was almost as bad. They looked through them. Or rather they looked at them but would not see who they really were. They refused to acknowledge the value of Māori culture or identity. Some of the settlers suffered from a form of almost fabulous vanity. There was no need to pay the natives for their land, one argument ran. Even reduced to pauperdom, living on the margins of their old property, Māori were repaid in full by the privilege of simply *looking at* the English. That way they would learn to be like them — and what greater treasure could fall from the sky? Left alone on vast reserves, Māori would not have engaged fully with European civilisation: it was therefore an act of kindness to relieve them of their property.

From here it was only a short step to conclude that no wrong could be found with the transaction. How to pierce this powerful self-delusion? This was the problem Ngāi Tahu faced. By 1879 their solution was clear. With complete composure, always calm and friendly, they focused on the facts of the case: what had been offered for sale, what was taken instead, what was promised in return and what was actually paid. They wrote down the answers, took them back to the pa and talked and talked into the night. *My sight did not penetrate at any time more than half way up the hall; for all we could see, it might have stretched away to boundless space and been crowded by countless Maoris.*

The reporter from Christchurch did not know it but just then he was in prophetic mode. In 1874, 1879, 1882, 1883, 1885, at Tuahiwi alone, great gatherings were held to discuss the land sale and the claim for justice. In 1868, 1879, 1881, 1886, 1891, 1906, 1921, 1925, 1929, 1944 — more hearings, reports, court cases, commissions, inquiries into inquiries into *Te Kerēme* —

The Claim. The Royal Commission of 1879 stayed several days in Kaiapoi then travelled to other towns for several months, and finally the commissioners delivered their findings: the tiny reserves granted by Mantell had been only a first instalment. But since no more reserves had been created, and since the other promises — for schools and hospitals — had not been kept, the Māori vendors were entitled to ten per cent of the profits on all subsequent sales of their property by the government. Plus accumulated interest.

The state therefore owed them £3 million.

'Simply absurd,' said the Minister of Lands, William Rolleston, who believed Māori should be a race of landless labourers. 'Not worth the paper it is written on.'

'Utterly impracticable,' said John Bryce, Minister of Native Affairs, who hated Māori and was cordially hated in return. 'A great mass of evidence has been taken and is lying in a box. It has never been read, and probably never will be.'

In 1886 a new Royal Commission was set up to review the findings of the 1879 Royal Commission. In 1887 a Joint Select Committee was set up to inquire into the new Royal Commission's inquiry into the previous Royal Commission. In 1889 a new committee was set up to reconsider the same evidence, rejecting the findings of both the 1879 Commission and the 1886 Commission.

It is hard to believe that for more than a hundred years, the government — 'the Crown' — which is no more than a number of politicians and civil servants who come on stage for a few years and walk up and down talking, mostly about the public good, then depart to be replaced by more of the same — carefully examined the facts of the Ngāi Tahu claim, generally agreed that a grave wrong had been committed, and then did very little about it.

It would be tedious to list all the cases, hearings, committees, commissions and acts of Parliament which followed, or the committees set up within Ngāi Tahu, the sub-committees and the rival sub-committees, which for a century or more repeatedly arrived at the same conclusions, and repeated the fact that they were the same, year after year.

Did anyone at the gatherings in the halls and meeting houses down dimly lit back roads of the South Island, talking about Te Kerēme decade after decade while their Pākehā fellow citizens were far away and fast asleep, think of the legend of Tāwera? *Te Hau . . . went one night to the foot of the hill, where there was a pool . . . This he completely covered with a network formed of saplings . . .* There is no way I can know, and perhaps it doesn't matter. Legends cast a pattern which people may follow without knowing. Archetypes are the patterns which reappear the most frequently, and defeat of the monster, the tyrant — *injustice* — is the most ancient archetype of all.

Finally, in this case, the monster began to weaken. It carried on fighting but lost its verve and conviction. The men and women who made up the Crown in 1990 could no longer think of anything to say. They were trapped in a network of facts written down and repeated for a hundred years. In 1998 they gave up the struggle. The word 'fail' tolls like a bell through the official apology. The Crown 'failed in most material respects to honour its obligations'; it 'failed to set aside adequate lands for Ngāi Tahu's use'; it 'failed to preserve and protect [such] land and valued possessions as they wished to retain'; it 'failed to act . . . reasonably and with the utmost good faith'.[26]

In 1882 a Māori MP, Hōne Mohi Tāwhai, stood up in Parliament and made a prediction. The Ngāi Tahu case was gradually being strengthened by each successive committee, he said, and if the present generation could not get justice, or the next two, 'probably the fourth would succeed'. How he made this calculation he didn't say. Perhaps it derived from memories of an old pattern in intertribal history — war, conquest, intermarriage, peace.

In Ngāi Tahu's case, Tāwhai was almost exactly on target. The official apology in 1998 was written into an act of Parliament which gave millions of dollars' worth of assets to Ngāi Tahu, especially fishing rights, and land including the highest peak in the country, Mount Cook, to which the ancient name brought from Polynesia — Aoraki — was restored, which carries a sense of the sunlit sublime, 'ao' being the personification of light and the upper world, and 'raki' (or rangi) the sky.

But the name also signals the other direction, down to earth, for Ao was a mythic being who once steered a great canoe, the South Island itself, into the heavens from where, as a result of certain regrettable mistakes, it came crashing to the ground, not unlike John Robert Godley's dream of an Oxonian England in the South Seas, or even Aoraki's own destiny not to be by far the highest mountain in the world at 15,000 metres, but settling instead for a modest 3700 metres, yet whose high roofbeam and the line of snowy alps you see when you come up the Fairlie road on a summer morning look as if constructed by the seraphim in the last five minutes.

Chapter 9

I knew none of the details of this story when Paddy and I
went for our stroll around the slopes of the Torlesse Range
and found the pool in the Kōwai. I knew the broad outlines:
an immense fraud, a century of both willed and unconscious
amnesia and then an abject apology, but it wasn't until I read
the history in some detail that I saw what really took place,
and the clearer it became the more puzzled I was. Why had it
happened at all? The South Island was so big and the number
of Māori so very small and the land so cheap it would have
been easy to reserve 1000 acres a head for every man, woman
and child of Ngāi Tahu iwi and hardly notice the difference.
And it would certainly have been simpler than the policy
chosen by 'Governor Hiccapenny', of fraud and threats and
then denials and fantasies of benevolence which lasted fifteen
decades. Why was that path taken?

The usual answer is 'racism', and perhaps that's true,

but the word is thrown around so readily today as a term of abuse it has lost all power to enlighten. In any case race relations are so complex and dynamic that the same one-word answer is not sufficient to diagnose the many causes of their breakdown. It was the French writer André Gide, visiting Africa in the 1920s, who noticed that the lower and worse the character of the white colonist, the lower and worse the Africans were in his or her judgement. In other words, another race is like a mirror which reflects your own character more clearly than anything else. And the mirror-image is inherently unstable, changing all the time as either party changes.

Transformations of this kind can be seen again and again in nineteenth-century New Zealand, where Europeans and Māori met more or less as strangers. When Walter Mantell, for instance, was engaged by the governor to rob Ngāi Tahu, he could find no words too strong to defame them in his diaries and letters — they were a *cunning, insolent, audaciously ignorant, turbulent, dishonest, sullen, evilly disposed* people who lived 'amidst spread straw, pigs, ducks, paintless boats and all imagined filth ad libitum'.

Yet when he completed his task of Extinguishing, almost to the hour, he completely changed his view. He *liked* Ngāi Tahu people. He admired them. He was sorry for what he had done. By the late 1850s he was writing to his former victims in tearful mode, signing himself 'your affectionate' or even 'your depressed brother'. There is no need to assume he was insincere. He spent the rest of his life making vague attempts to redress the wrongs he had done. He admitted that he had participated in 'a disreputable fraud' in 1848 in order to further his own career. He intended to put things right later.

On the cover of the sketchbook he took with him on his journey of Extinguishing, he wrote: *Non si male nunc et olim sic erit neque semper . . .* ('If things are bad now, they won't always be'). But Mantell could not put things right later. We are changed by our deeds. He defrauded Māori, trapping them in tiny reserves surrounded by Pākehā-owned land and laws, then he found he was trapped himself. 'I had no idea in those days,' he said once, 'when I was sent for and requested to compel the natives . . . to come under a deed from which they derived no benefit . . . I had no idea of the great amount of self-reproach I was laying in store for myself.'[27] Perhaps, though, he did have some idea.

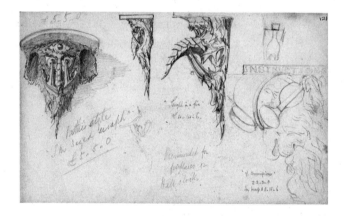

In the same sketchbook there is a page with a self-portrait made during the journey, grinning in the lower right-hand corner, and three peculiar grotesques which depict a kind of wall-bracket or capital which is also alive, a demon — the '3-eyed seraph' he calls it — with pouring tears and a drooping beak. This has the authentic look of a face seen in a very bad dream, and later in life, ensconced in power in Wellington — at one point he became Minister of Native Affairs — Mantell was overcome by a strange inertia whenever he tried to make amends for his actions in the South Island. Filled with sorrow and self-reproach, he nevertheless became suddenly venomous again, and unable to move a limb.

'Depressed' Walter Mantell is therefore a ludicrous figure, like the Carpenter on the beach sobbing over the fate of the Oysters, and while Lewis Carroll, writing *Alice Through the Looking Glass* in his rooms in Christ Church, Oxford, must have known of the new Christchurch with its own quadrangles and rose gardens on the other side of the world, and perhaps even had it in mind as a location for Wonderland ('Excuse me, Ma'am,' says Alice, practising a curtsey in mid-air as she

'O Oysters, come and walk with us!'
The Walrus did beseech.
'A pleasant walk, a pleasant talk,
Along the briny beach:

falls down the rabbit hole, 'is this New Zealand or Australia?'),
whether he followed the actual course of events there or ever
heard of such a person as Walter Mantell is not something that
has been ascertained.

The transformative arc can also be seen clearly in the case
of Charlotte Godley, the wittiest and most snobbish of the
colonists writing home to their mothers in the 1850s. Her
father was MP for Caernarvonshire, as was his father before
him and his before him — wealthy Tory squires, they had
represented Caernarvonshire at Westminster since Tudor
times or perhaps the Flood — and Charlotte sailed from
England in 1849 with all the prejudices of her caste.

'Some of them [Māori],' she writes, 'and especially the
women, are frightful, but they look very picturesque, sitting
about the place with a bright scarlet blanket and a deep black
border spread all over them . . . They really seem as if their
only natural position was squatting, for nothing else describes
it, with their chin on their knees and a pipe in their mouths . . .

'The men are generally better looking, and better dressed
too . . . I was among their huts . . . bargaining for some melons
which I thought would be acceptable presents on board, when
a great tall man came home from his work, in a straw hat, and
blanket tied round his waist; which he immediately proceeded
to take off, leaving only a very small garment behind . . . I
was near taking to my heels; but the next moment saw him
down with the others, rolled like a ball in his blanket, by the
fire in front of the huts, and his mouth full of hot potatoes;
the women crawling about and screaming out their uncouth
words. It was getting dark, and with firelight glimmering on
the whole scene . . . to me it was like a dream, indeed I often

feel inclined to say, like the old woman in the story, "if I be I, as I suppose I be".'[28]

Three months later, there are signs not that Charlotte Godley's views had changed but that they might be subject to change: 'Wellington. The natives are, on the whole, both better and worse than I expected. That is, some are quite good looking, civilized-looking people; among the men, very well dressed and more like ourselves in colour, size and bearing, than the Lascars or any *coloured* people that I have seen. Most of the large "stores" have them as servants, and the Police are mostly Maoris and are a very efficient and well-drilled body . . . But when you see them in their wild state and dress, squatting about in their *pahs* (villages) . . . all scrambling together for potatoes and Indian corn in some wood ashes on the open ground. At the same time, you hear many stories proving that they have a strong sense of religion, and other good feelings; but they have no word for thank-you in their language . . .'

A week or two on, in Ōtaki, about 80 kilometres north of Wellington: 'I never saw anything nicer than the way in which the natives came flocking out to meet Mr Hadfield . . . We had to pass quite through the village to get to the house we were to sleep in, which turned out to be a very pretty little reed cottage . . . so well built as to be a beautiful specimen of *the style* . . . [B]efore the house [was] a round hole about a foot deep, such as they use for ovens and fireplaces; and by this we sat on the ground, wrapped in blankets like themselves . . . Some of the men, and one of the women, were very good-looking. I wish you could have seen the group round that fire, with the bright blaze . . . lighting up such picturesque wild-looking faces.'

Another week passes. The Godleys are now back in Wellington: 'Thompson, our dear Maori chief, from Otaki came to tell us that, as Archdeacon Williams was going home to England for two years, he had suddenly made up his mind to go with him, and see all that he can . . . I hope he will arrive while you are in London. I should be so glad that you should see him . . . I am sure you would like him . . . He and his wife have been dining with us to-day, and so we gave, for us, quite a grand banquet. Arthur and I spent a very hot hour in picking gooseberries for a large tart . . . Then we had roast beef, and a coursed rabbit, the finest I ever saw . . . and some artichokes that Colonel McCleverty had sent us; [the guests] were much amused by nibbling the leaves. Thompson, in putting pepper on them, upset some over his plate, on which Mrs Thompson burst out laughing, and said, in Maori of course, that if he did that in England the "pakehas" would laugh, and think him very vulgar.'

Whatever is going on here, it is not 'racism' in any usual or useful sense of the word. Charlotte was a tremendous snob: most of the settlers she met in New Zealand she would never have dreamt of sending to see her mother in Portman Square but 'our dear Maori chief' (Tāmihana Te Rauparaha, son of the great Ngāti Toa leader Te Rauparaha) was quite acceptable. It was only a few weeks after dining on gooseberry tart and artichokes with Tāmihana and his wife that the Godleys went riding through the tussocks of the as yet nonexistent Christchurch and, camping in the bush at Rangiora, dined on *infantine* potatoes with Ngāi Tahu.

South Island Māori, in other words, were not cheated of their land because they were hated or despised as a people, which is to say because of racism, but for another reason. It was because they could be. It was too easy. It was a question of power. Ngāi Tahu were vastly outnumbered by the British, had no way to fend them off and at the same time were fearful of losing the mana over their land, which included their right to sell it. Young Torlesse was right when he wrote to his mother that Ngāi Tahu were to be mistreated — 'neglected' was his word — because they were few in number, and without military power.

The conclusion is not a happy one. The urge of the strong to oppress the weak — the nuns and the orphans, the older orphans and the younger, George Moore and the swagman, the white mob and the black men in Marion, Walter Mantell and Ngāi Tahu — is so powerful that at times nothing in the world, not the US Constitution or the Sermon on the Mount or the most precise *Instructions* from the Secretary of State for the Colonies, can overcome it.

We were still in the pool of the Kōwai, Paddy and I, under the high crags outlined against the late morning sun. With the heat glaring off the rocks around us it was hard to leave the water, but there was Paddy's programme to consider. So far we had approached the Torlesse Range from the east and then the south. Now he wanted to drive west and look at it from there, and so reluctantly we got out, dried off almost instantly — I watched my wet footprints vanish from the rock in seconds — and in half a minute, by the time we had gone around the corner and down the valley, there would have been no more sign we had ever been there than there was that Torlesse and Tuwhia once hurried past, or that Metehau, owner of Tāwera, took the same route into the heart of those mountains, which presumably he did at some point in his life. But looking back later, I thought it was the nearest we came to our quarry that day: in the dazzle of noon it was easy to imagine the particle-flash of the legend, a giant bird rushing down to a shallow pool where Te Hau o Tāwera and 50 men lay hiding and in wait.

We came back to the highway, closed the five-barred gate behind us and drove away. Climbing west and over a pass, we came out once again into a completely different landscape. A wide valley, semi-arable, neatly fenced, sheep grazing on pumpkins . . . it was almost a domestic scene, except that on the skyline there stood a strange assembly of rocks, all natural formations but looking like the stubble of some forgotten civilisation. This, Paddy said, was named Kura Tawhiti, although Kura Tawhiti is also the name of one of the mountains behind us which Metehau claimed, and whether the mountain took its name from the rocks or the rocks from the mountain is not known.

The name means 'treasure from afar' and the treasure is usually taken to mean the kūmara, the sweet potato brought by early Māori settlers to New Zealand and apparently grown in gardens among these protecting stones. But there was also a completely different tradition, Paddy told me, which states that the treasure was not a potato but a whole body of traditional lore — spiritual, genealogical, astronomical, agricultural — which had also been brought across the Pacific and was then taught for many generations among the rocks and caves on the hill. The higher the learning attained by the students, the higher up the hillside they were led the following year.

This school of learning, or wānanga, had been convened by the Waitaha, the first people to settle in the South Island (although shadowy predecessors, the Hāwea and the Rapuwai, are sometimes mentioned), but students from other tribes or iwi were allowed to attend. The Waitaha lived undisturbed in their island for probably three centuries but were eventually displaced (killed, enslaved, driven away or assimilated) by invaders from the north, Ngāti Mamoe, and two centuries later the Mamoe were dismissed by another North Island force, Ngāi Tahu, who then fell out among themselves and, weakened by civil strife, were attacked by yet another northern tribe, Ngāti Toa Rangatira. They were just getting their breath back when the British arrived from the other side of the world and took their land.

All this, which Paddy outlined in about three minutes, constituted the entire human history of the South Island, as far as is known, and was so at odds with the monumental calm of the valley, the standing stones in the distance and the

mountains asleep behind them, that it seemed quite unreal:
the island, after all, being so big and the number of people
living there at any time so small, it must have often been hard
to find your enemy, or even find someone to *be* your enemy.

We didn't stay long. Kura Tawhiti was not on Paddy's
agenda that day and we drove on another few kilometres,
turned right into a carpark and then set out on a walk across
rough open country. The Torlesse Range had dwindled in the
distance and looked compact and complete and oddly bare,
yet also revelatory — one mountain was all scree, and another
had an odd reddish tinge — like stage scenery which is seen
from behind only by the actors and stagehands. And then
suddenly, about a kilometre away across a chasm, was the last
thing either of us expected. A truly giant eagle . . .

It was only another natural formation and it goes without
mention in the guidebooks, but it looked so like a great bird
of prey perched on a ridge and gazing towards Tāwera that —

first of all — it made us laugh, being at the same time wholly unlikely and perfectly apt. Then it struck me that this great artefact of the wind and rain might be evidence not that the legend of Te Hau o Tāwera was true, but the opposite.

There is no doubt that Waitaha and other early arrivals must have engaged in desperate struggles with the giant eagle at different times and in different places, but over the years perhaps the stories were reduced and concentrated into one, in one location, here 'below a spur of Tawera', because of the presence of this 'image', around which a legend might circle and settle and, folding its wings, look up at a wild imagined nest.

Chapter 10

The sun had set by the time we got back to Christchurch but it was still light enough, Paddy decreed, to go and see the sights, the main sights in Christchurch in 2013 being the earthquake damage in the centre of the city. We came in past the airport and around Park Terrace where George Moore once sat in his mansion in the dark, passed Canterbury Museum built by Julius von Haast, parked the car and walked along Worcester Street until we were stopped by a barrier of cyclone fencing. Beyond that was the 'red zone', the heart of the city still closed to the public. It was Saturday night, but nothing was moving in there. A bulldozer was parked aslant on a pile of white rubble. The red dome of the Regent Cinema was lying weirdly intact but upside down in the street.

The cathedral was still there in the dusk but something terrible had happened to it — I thought I could see a glimpse of sky below the eaves where there should be masonry and of course the spire had gone. I knew already that the spire had fallen — it was the first thing mentioned in the newsflash after the 2011 quake. I was in Auckland at the time, driving across town on a steamy summer day, white clouds floating up over the ridgelines, when the phone rang: 'Big quake in Christchurch just now,' someone said, 'the *spire* is down.' I knew exactly which spire she meant and for a moment the centrepiece of Godley's dream-city served another purpose: to register the scale of the earth's movement by falling down with a roar.

All the same, two years later — to *see* it not there in the semi-darkness . . . along with other familiar things not there as well. The *Press* building, for instance, with its prim little cupola, like the tone of its editorials, seemed to have gone, and what about the cinemas — the Tivoli, and the State with its Art Deco façade, and the Avon with its lovely green neon sign like a mild waterfall, and Warners Hotel and the United Services where the Queen once stayed? Perhaps some had been knocked down long ago. I knew that for years Christchurch had suffered serious vandalism in the name of 'development'.

But it was the absence of the spire that shook me most. It felt like a personal loss. This was odd because although in my childhood the cathedral spire stood at the centre of my idea of the grown-up world, the neon-lit cinemas, the best hotels and the offices where my father worked, I had never liked it much. I was too young to judge its architectural merit but as a ten-year-old, looking up, I used to think it had a lofty, sleepy, disdainful air — that it didn't like *me* very much, a kid from a Catholic school in a sky-blue cap and blazer —

for the cathedral was not just centre and symbol of the city but of a markedly Protestant and almost officially Anglican city. This was at a time when sectarian differences were much more important than they are now, and in fact, apart from gradations of wealth, which mattered there as they do everywhere, the Protestant–Catholic divide was the only one we ever noticed in flat, white, largely egalitarian Christchurch.

In the part of town where I lived there was no hint of racial division mainly because the Māori population there was almost nonexistent, but there was also no indication there had ever been racial differences in the district or even any interracial history at all. I grew up in Papanui, in the north of the city; every summer my mother would load the car with kids on the hottest days and drive us a few miles up the road to swim in the Waimakariri, in the cold, glacier-green pools under willows not far from the bridge, and perhaps once a year the whole family would go on a longer drive for a picnic at Ashley Gorge, where Charlotte Godley saw 'a good sized river [coming] through a deep-wooded rent in the rocks'.

The Waimakariri and the Ashley were the boundaries, north and south, of the Ngāi Tahu heartland, the Waimakariri block, but we didn't know that for we never heard the term or knew such a thing had existed, and if there was ever vague mention of a distant, long-dead relation, the Rev. John Raven, who lived north of the river and who was the man who gathered up and buried the bones of the warriors at Kaiapoi which had been lying in the sun and rain for decades, it never crossed our minds to wonder what he was doing with a farm in Ngāi Tahu's heartland in the first place.

Every year, our school picnic was held at Woodend Beach

141

and coaches were parked in the Woodend Domain, very near if not on the exact spot where Walter Mantell stood on a sandhill and announced the theft of millions of acres of land from Ngāi Tahu, but none of us, as we raced off into the pines and through the dunes to the beach, knew that either, for none of us had ever heard of Mantell, much less of Metehau.

There was a peculiar custom at our school relating to this picnic. The day before, out of sight and knowledge of the teachers, the boys formed an army. No one knew where this tradition had come from but it went unquestioned. We gathered at the far side of the playing fields by an alley of short and always rather mealy-leaved poplars, and a certain boy who had appointed himself general then announced the rest of our ranks.

His name was Warwick Ison, and here was another mystery because for the rest of the year Warwick was rather anonymous — middle of the class, middling at sports, unmarked by any distinction — but on the day before the picnic at Woodend he acquired supreme authority. From where? No one asked. Perhaps we were responding to some atavistic Anglo-Saxon urge: we were about to go into the wilderness, 500 acres of pines and dunes in Woodend Domain: we should be prepared to seize and hold it by force.

During mobilisation, the day before the picnic, Warwick adopted a peculiar mannerism which I have rarely seen since. After each announcement of rank was made — 'Smith, Colonel', it might be, or 'Brown, Lieutenant' — Warwick would close his eyes for a few seconds, then open them again before proceeding to the next one. And we all knew what this impressive remonstration meant. '*My decision is final.*'

But then — and this was the third mystery — as soon as we arrived at Woodend we raced away into the pines and the sandhills, and Warwick, the army, and all our ranks and orders were completely forgotten.

I wasn't thinking of Warwick that night, as Paddy and I stood looking through the cyclone fence at the half-fallen cathedral down the street, but he was to come to mind later. In the meantime Paddy, nothing if not meticulous, drove us around to the north side of Cathedral Square and we looked in at it again, and saw piles of rubble, white as sugar, and the crumbled base of the tower, and the plinth from which a bronze statue of Godley had fallen forward on its face, just as a marble statue of Rolleston, the Minister of Lands who laughed at Ngāi Tahu's claims of injustice, had fallen on its back and lost its head along the street.

Then Paddy drove over to the east side of the city and we looked through the darkness, now nearly complete, at the ruins of the Catholic basilica, where an avalanche of broken

masonry had burst in among the classical orders under the dome, while the dome itself, also weirdly intact, was lying upside down on the ground outside. And later that night, when I was falling asleep at my cousin's house in south Christchurch, an image came to me of the dark central city a few kilometres away and it looked like the tablecloth of the Mad Hatter's Tea Party, littered with broken eggshells, spilled sugar, crumbled cake and fallen salt cellars.

This was not the first time I had thought of Lewis Carroll while I was in Canterbury, and later, after I had left, when I read the stories of Mantell and Metehau and saw how the whole landscape of my childhood — school grounds, picnic grounds, city streets, the plains and hills and mountains — had all been taken in what Mantell later described as a 'disreputable fraud', I also re-read Lewis Carroll who at the same time had been sitting in his rooms in Christ Church, Oxford, writing of a world where a cat may vanish while its smile stays hanging in the air and a lion and a unicorn fight in a dark wood and a troop of soldiers turn into playing cards and blow away in the wind. For that reason, I suppose, I was able to take half seriously the idea that as a boy, when I was looking up at the cathedral, it had an 'expression' I didn't like, and then I thought of Warwick Ison again and I thought, 'But I was wrong about what the expression meant.'

It was nothing to do with sectarian differences between Catholics and Protestants. High above the city streets and looking out over the plains as far as the mountains, all taken by a fraud not redressed for 150 years, that was the real meaning I read in those lofty, sleepy, downturned louvres above my head: *The decision is final.*

The next morning in south Christchurch I woke early. No one else was up so I decided to walk around the corner to a bakery I had seen the night before and buy rolls and croissants for the household. It was very quiet outside — Sunday morning, tree shadows still long across the footpaths and not a soul to be seen, even when I reached Colombo Street, which runs in a straight line north to south for several miles through the city. I started to think I must have imagined the bakery in the next block since there was no one coming or going there, and then, as I walked across the street to check, something caught my eye and I thought, *I've never seen that before.*

I stopped to look again, and realised that not only had I never seen it before from there but for about a hundred years no one else had either: far away to the north, beyond the city limits, beyond the Waimakariri, beyond the hills of Glenmark, was a single conical mountain, delicately lit by the rising sun, and I knew it could not have been seen from there before because the tower and spire of the cathedral had been deliberately built forward a few feet on Colombo Street to dominate the town from one end to the other and would have blocked the view.[29]

But the spire was gone now and the single mountain, faint and clear in the early eastern light, seemed like an image of the land before the British arrived, and before the Māori arrived, and perhaps even before *Harpagornis* arrived, and then this idea, of a far-off and pristine past, made me think as I walked along the footpath to the bakery — which I saw was open because two or three coloured fly-screen ribbons just then fluttered at the door — of a far-off and perhaps pristine

future when all the events in this part of the book, from
Te Hau o Tāwera's battle with an eagle to a city falling down
in a cloud of dust, will be completely forgotten or at most a
few brief lines, compact and baffling, like the records we have
from a time when there were only a few cities in the world and
none of them were old.

III

Meadows of Gold

Chapter 11

In the year 947 AD a new history of the world was published in Baghdad, then the greatest city on Earth, the 'place of peace', circular in form and surrounded by gardens and canals fed from the Euphrates, and beyond that an empire, the Caliphate, which at its zenith included Arabia, Persia and Egypt. *The Meadows of Gold and Mines of Gems* was written by a certain al-Masudi, who had travelled widely in Muslim lands, from the Caspian Sea in the north to Ceylon in the east and possibly as far as Zanzibar, and who also reported on places further off, occasionally noting activity in a dark corner of the world no one knew much about, western Europe.

In Volume IV of *Meadows of Gold* the following story appears: 'In the first ages of the world, God created a bird of marvellous beauty, bestowing on him all the perfections: a face like a human being, resplendent feathers of the richest colours, wings on each of his four limbs, his hands armed with claws, and the end of his beak as solid as that of an eagle. God created a female bird in the image of the male and gave the couple the name *Anqa*. He then revealed his plan to Moses, son of Amran: "I have given you a creature of the most wonderful form, I have made both male and female, I have allowed them to prey on the wild animals which live around Jerusalem, and now I wish to establish friendship between you and these beings as proof of the supremacy you have been granted among the children of Israel."

'Soon after, Moses and the Jews were led by God into the wilderness . . . and it was then that the Anqa abandoned the wilderness for the lands of Arabia where it devoured children, and flocks, and savage beasts. Finally, during the interval which separates Jesus from Mahomet, a prophet named Khaled, the son of Sinan, appeared among the tribes there,

and, moved by the sorrow of those people whose children were decimated by the Anqa, he prayed to God to extirpate this race of birds.

'And then God made them perish.'

The story was already old when al-Masudi wrote it down, and seems to have a pre-Islamic origin. It probably started as a Jewish tale inspired by images, from a much more ancient period of Mesopotamian history, of the griffin-demons such as Anzu or Imdugud, or their offspring consorting amiably with Assyrian kings. These marvellous creatures had evidently existed once but were no longer to be found. They must have misbehaved and been punished with death.

Another version of the story is specific about the crime: 'The Anqa used to live among men and caused affliction to living creatures until, in the time of Hanzala, who lived between Jesus and Mohammed, it carried off a bride with her jewels and robes. Hanzala prayed . . . "O Lord, take it and cut off its progeny and bear hardly upon it with calamity."

'God (*may He be exalted!*) sent a fire which burnt it, and nothing remained but the name.'[1]

In a Persian version of the tale, the Anqa is replaced by the Simurgh, but again evil behaviour brings about its downfall: 'It is said it [the Simurgh] has disappeared since the time of Solomon the prophet because of what it said: *"I will change the decrees of eternal destiny."* Solomon . . . had informed it that on that same day a daughter had been born to the King of the East, and a son to the King of the West, and that it was fated that they should come together. The Simurgh went and carried off the daughter of the King of the East and took her to his own nest and brought her up. It chanced that the son of the King of the West took a desire to travel and happened on the place. The daughter fell in love with him and devised a scheme whereby the youth hid inside the skin of an animal which had died . . . At her request the Simurgh brought her the skin, and the two came together and had a child. Then . . . the mystery became known, and the Simurgh disappeared from amongst men, because of the shame of it.'[2]

The most important thing about the *Meadows of Gold* version is its attribution. Al-Masudi put it in the mouth of Ibn Abbas, the young cousin and 'shadow' of the Prophet Mohammed. And not only that: Ibn Abbas, according to al-Masudi, ascribes the legend to Mohammed himself. ('One day the Prophet told us . . .')

This strange tale, in other words, comes into view inside two sets of quotation marks which give it a certain authority. It does not appear in the Qu'ran but is among the Hadith, the body of stories and commentaries which have gathered around the Qu'ran, and in a sense it is a semi-sacred tale, attributed to the Prophet and not something to be tampered with lightly.

Then, in the eleventh century, there is a remarkable change. In a commentary on religion *Rabi' al-Abrar* ('The Spring of the Pious') a Persian writer named Zamakhshari retells the story: 'In the era of the Jews, God created near Jerusalem a bird with a face like that of a man, which they called Anqa and which used to harass other creatures. The prophet of that age prayed and God threw it into the Ocean, south of the Equator, and from that time onwards it disappeared.'

Zamakhshari was famous for his piety and careful attention to form. When he was a young man he lost a foot through frostbite and for the rest of his life carried around a notarised statement to that effect, in case people thought his foot had been cut off as punishment for a crime. He was also a careful logician, and is still regarded as a heretic in the stricter schools of Islam: while accepting that the Qu'ran was the word of God he would not agree it was *co-eternal* with the deity. The author, he thought, might be allowed to precede his own writings.

His scruples are what make Zamakhshari interesting. He was not the sort of writer who would change a venerable, semi-sacred tale out of zest for novelty. Where did this notion come from, of the Anqa's exile 'into the Ocean, south of the Equator'? The change is remarkable, though still cautious. The writer does not say the Anqa is alive but nor is it definitely dead. It 'disappeared' in a particular zone, which is almost impossible to reach but a real place all the same. Could this variation to the story indicate that rumours have now reached the Middle East that a great bird, as beautiful and dangerous as the Anqa of the legend, has been sighted in a land which no one knows anything about?

It comes as a surprise today, when the superiority of Islamic civilisation over mediaeval Europe is often emphasised, to realise how little advanced from the rest of the world the Middle East was. Baghdad was a many-domed city with splendid libraries, schools of jurisprudence and hundreds of bookshops, yet even the great traveller al-Masudi knew nothing about most of the planet. Arab cosmography and geography at the time were the same as that of India. 'The Earth is like an egg floating in water' was a common description. In other words there was a single landmass — Africa and Eurasia — surrounded by a belt of navigable sea scattered with islands, and beyond that lay the *moheet*, the Circumambient, the Great Encircling Ocean, where no man could travel and where demons and jinn existed, and also the Antichrist, in whom the Islamic world firmly believed.

The Atlantic was known of in Baghdad, but it was *mare tenebrosum* — the sea of shadows where the sun went down. Nothing good could be hoped for there. Even the nearby Mediterranean was uncanny: 'The Western Sea of Rum,' wrote al-Muqadassi in the ninth-century book *The Pleasure of Hearts*, 'is 2500 leagues in length, here 200 leagues in breadth, and there 500. The southern shores are in Muslim hands but the other side is occupied by the Christians. It is a difficult and tempestuous body of water and a loud and continuous noise is heard at all times in it, but particularly on Thursday nights.'

Particularly Thursday nights . . . In a great city like Baghdad, of course, there were people of more sceptical temper who probably did not believe in the Anqa or the Simurgh or noisy Thursday nights. I am thinking of al-Jahiz, one of the rare figures who make the cliché come true and do seem to step forth from the pages of history. Everything about him was unusual for a celebrated writer: his grandfather was a slave, he was poor, as a young man he sold fish for a living, he was 'goggle-eyed'. You see this clever, ill-favoured young African running a fish stall beside a canal in Basra. His intelligence flickers like fire across the distance. A millennium before Darwin he intuited evolution: 'Animals engage in a struggle for existence, to eat and avoid being eaten and to breed. Environmental factors influence organisms to develop new characteristics to ensure survival, thus transforming them into new species. Those that survive pass on their successful characteristics to their offspring.'[3]

He wrote a treatise on black Africans, the Zanj: 'There is no people on earth in whom generosity is so universally developed as the Zanj, no better singers, no people more polished and eloquent and less given to insulting language, they are courageous, energetic and generous which are the virtues of nobility . . . White and black are the results of environment, the distance from the sun and intensity of heat. There is no question of metamorphosis, or of punishment, disfigurement or favour meted out by Allah.'

Al-Jahiz also turned his mind to the problem of evil: 'Pure evil would mean the end of the world but if good were undiluted, the testing required of us would be meaningless and there would be no need to take thought.' This is not quite orthodox. Knowledge, and knowledge (i.e. experience) of good and evil, were separate things before the Fall. It was only afterwards they became entangled: humanity now had to think its way through endless problems. But thinking was still a distinguished act:

'Without thought, wisdom ceases . . . discrimination disappears, there is no certainty, no hesitation, no studying, no science . . . angels and men return to the condition of beasts, to the condition of the heavenly bodies, lower even than grazing animals. For who would be content to be the sun, the moon, fire or snow, a tower or a wisp of cloud or even the whole Milky Way, and not take thought?'

Not many minds reach this consideration: Al-Jahiz would rather have been al-Jahiz, selling fish beside a seawater canal, than the sun.

As to the legendary bird, the Anqa, al-Jahiz turns the question around. He does not deny its existence but merely asks questions. 'Tell me about the *anqa muhgrib*. What were its father and mother? Was it created by the union of male and female? When does it make a cradle for its child, when does it cover the imam's supporters with its wings and when does have a bridle put upon its back?'

In other words, nothing is known. There are only enquiries, elegant and ironic. Perhaps al-Jahiz had read the Book of Job, where the questions have the same ring. 'Hast thou entered into the treasures of the snow or hast thou seen the treasures of the hail? Dost thou know the balancings of the clouds?' The answer is, frankly, no. But whatever the writers of eighth-, ninth- and tenth-century Baghdad thought about the Anqa or the Simurgh — that they never existed, or once existed and then perished — they agreed on one thing: they would not be seen anymore. Then came Zamakhshari, announcing that the Anqa had not necessarily been destroyed: it had been sent away to a place far across the ocean and below the equator.

More information was soon to hand. A few years later, in 1162, a new book appeared, *Tuhfat al-Albab*, or the 'Gift of Secrets and Selection of Wonders'. The writer, Abu Hamid al-Gharnati, states: 'Among the islands of the China Seas there exists a bird which is known as the Ruhkh . . . There arrived in the Maghreb [North Africa] a man who had been a trader by sea to China. He lived there for a time and then returned to the Maghreb with great wealth and a feather of the ruhkh. The wind had carried them away to a great island. The crew disembarked to take on wood and water. Then they saw a great dome. It was the egg of the ruhkh and 100 cubits high.

They beat it, and out came a chicken of the ruhkh. They killed it and cooked it . . . When the sun rose they saw the ruhkh coming towards them together with its mate and in its talons a piece of rock and as it approached the ship it threw the rock but the ship was moving fast and it survived.'

Al-Gharnati or, to give him his full name, Abu Hamid Muhammad ibn Abd al-Rahman ibn Suleiman al Mazini ibn Rabi al-Qaysi al Gharnati, was cut from a different cloth from the cautious Zamakhshari, and there is almost nothing in his story that doesn't stretch credibility. Yet two assertions stand out as possible facts: the island of the Rukh was in the China Seas.

From an Arab perspective 'China Seas' meant all the ocean to the east and south-east of China. Secondly, it is clearly stated, perhaps for the first time in writing, that someone from the Middle East has sailed out into this great ocean and come back to tell the tale.

The story above, of course, is now familiar to everyone. It is almost identical to the tale of the Fifth Voyage of Sindbad. It appears in *The Arabian Nights*, in fact, not once but twice, told by the concubine Scheherazade. The first version begins on Night Four Hundred and Four, breaking with the famous formula 'But then Scheherazade saw the first light of dawn, and discreetly fell silent' — a formula which kept the story alive and kept Scheherazade alive as well, unlike other concubines who spent the night with the Sultan and were murdered in the morning.

There is an old motif here — spinning out a tale to stave off death, or at least ill-temper. In the Hindu *Romance of the Aerial Spirits*, compiled hundreds of years earlier, the gender roles were reversed. The god Shiva sits with his wife, the Daughter of the Mountain: 'In a burst of affection the Moon-Crested God, alert to her praises, put her on his lap and said "What can I do for you?" She asked for a story, but it displeased her, and to restore her good humour Shiva promised his wife another, and he then proceeded to tell her The Romance of the Aerial Spirits.'

The Romance or *Great Narrative* ran to thousands of stories and form the vast cycle known today as *The Ocean of the Rivers of Story*; we only have a seventh of the original text, but even that is twice the length of the *Iliad* and the *Odyssey* combined.

The Arabian Nights is terse by comparison. The arrival of the dawn, however, to pause the story was a brilliant innovation. Only rarely does daylight break in the Western literature to the same effect — sunrise as intermission. *A Midsummer Night's Dream* ends with the 'iron tongue of midnight' — a signal for silence and deep sleep. In Castiglione's *The Book of the Courtier*, the most famous book in the sixteenth century, the revels do last till dawn, and for four nights in a row a group of people, mostly young, stay up late in the palace of Urbino, talking, laughing, discussing love, sport, politics. Especially politics: 'Of all the calamities that can come to a country, none is worse than a bad man in power, for all the others — strife, plague and war — follow in his footsteps.'

Finally, at the end of the fourth night, the conversations end.

'"We'll meet again tonight," someone says.

'"How can it be tonight?" quoth the Duchesse.

'"Because it is day already," said Lord Cesare, and he showed her the light that began to enter in at the clefts of the windows. And they all stood looking in wonder.'[4]

The year was 1507. It was a high point of the Renaissance. 'Perhaps in future centuries there will be some few who envy us ours,' says one of the group. In fact they never meet again to continue the conversation, or at least not in Castiglione's book, which ends there, the windows open on 'dawn the colour of a rose, all the stars voided . . . and a cold wind blowing from the wood'.[5]

Castiglione spent more than 20 years perfecting his account of conversations in Urbino and must have decided that four nights were enough. In *The Arabian Nights*, interruption by the rising sun recurs hundreds of times — the number has varied in different editions over the centuries — and it never loses its power, like dawn itself, ancient as the Earth yet always new. In *The Arabian Nights* there is an additional element, of terror. The *Nights* is a murder story, or a story of murder narrowly avoided. Sunrise is a time of terror. Only the story brings safety, as long as it is unfinished.

Scheherazade knows this and the sultan knows what she is up to and he will still kill her if she finishes the tale and doesn't start another. A sense of dread, quite absent from *Courtier*, hangs over the frame story from the Middle East. Nobody knows the identity of the original author, who may well have been a woman. By guile, and fiction, which is in any case the art of withholding information, Scheherazade civilises a murderous ruler.

On Night Four Hundred and Five, then, she completes the story about the strange island where huge birds swoop down on human visitors. But she tells the same story on Night Five Hundred and Sixty-five. This time there is no man from the Maghreb. This version is entitled The Fifth Voyage of Sindbad the Sailor. No one knows exactly when Sindbad first appeared in literature. He did not originally belong in *The Arabian Nights.* His stories were inserted there — although perhaps not for the first time — by the French in the earliest European edition published in the eighteenth century.

The oldest extant manuscript of the Sindbad stories is in seventeenth-century Turkish but the Sindbad cycle is much older than that, and is generally thought to have been compiled in the eleventh or early twelfth century in Baghdad. Whatever the date, it was clear to Professor Bivar that Sindbad's Second Voyage and Fifth Voyage derived from the same source that al-Gharnati used for the story about the man from the Maghreb, whose ship was blown out into the China Seas. An uninhabited land, a large white egg, the shadow of a huge, angry parent bird flying overhead . . .

Despite the fabulous exaggerations, al-Gharnati, like Zamakhshari, was not primarily in the business of making things up. He regarded himself as a kind of scientist. His book, the *Tuhfat,* was one of many 'wonder books' whose purpose was to describe the natural world accurately. Whoever compiled the stories of Sindbad was under no such restraint. His — or her — work was an entertainment, and fantastic tales migrated from ancient Egypt, India, Greece, Persia and China. Sindbad has definite predecessors in the Hindu *Romance of the Aerial Spirits*, castaways who also creep among the feathers of a great bird to be carried away to other lands. In order to use recent information about a giant bird now named the Rukh and said to be living in the 'China Seas', the writer of the Sindbad cycle had to drop the man from the Maghreb. In all seven of the tales, Sindbad is a restless resident of Baghdad who repeatedly goes to sea.

Yet it seems clear that a real traveller, a 'man from the Maghreb', did once exist. Another Baghdad writer, named al-Jawzi, even says he met him in person. This was reported much later by an historian named al-Wardi in one of his own books, *The Pearl of Wonders and Uniqueness of Strange Things*. Al-Wardi tells us that the encounter was described by al-Jawzi in a zoological treatise. Unfortunately, al-Jawzi was the most prolific writer in Arab history — he wrote at least 700 books, and many have not been translated and some are lost, so the treatise in question has not been identified.

On the other hand, al-Jawzi was famous and we know a lot about him. He was witty, handsome, charming and loquacious; at the age of ten he made a speech to 50,000 people and after that never stopped emitting words in one form or another. He wrote so much without re-reading it, it was said, that no one ever relied on a thing he said but they loved him all the same. Half the population of Baghdad followed his bier to the grave in tears.

His last words, his grandson reported, were to some invisible bedside visitors: 'What do you want me to do with these peacocks?' Did al-Jawzi see himself just then walking away into a walled garden, a 'paradise', or was this a pious story made up to give that impression? Either way, we know the precise moment of al-Jawzi's death — 'just before the red of sunset was leaving the sky' on the night before the 13th of Ramadan 597 AH, which is 14 June 1201 CE. He was 85. If he really did meet a traveller, a man from the Maghreb, perhaps as a boy meeting a very old man, who told him that he had sailed out into the Great Encircling Ocean, found a land ruled by a terrifying bird, and then managed to get home again, that sea voyage might have taken place any time after about 1070, which is more or less the time that the first reports are emerging that the Anqa had not been destroyed by fire or any other means, but was exiled in the ocean below the equator.

That story was in circulation in the Middle East by 1160, according to three versions which have come down to us — in the *Tuhfat*, the Sindbad cycle, and *The Arabian Nights*. But where in the Great Encircling Ocean was this purported landfall? As well as the reference to 'the China Seas' in al-Gharnati's version, there are certain geographical clues in *The Arabian Nights*. Here is Richard Burton's 1885 translation of Sindbad's Second Voyage, as told on Night Five Hundred and Forty-three: 'At last Destiny brought us to an island fair and verdant, in trees abundant, with yellow-ripe fruits luxuriant, and flowers fragrant and birds warbling soft descant; and streams crystalline and radiant; but no sign of man showed to the descrier, no, not a blower of the fire.'

A land of flowing stream and flowering trees sounds like a generic Arabian paradise, but two precise geographical indicators are also here. 'Not a blower of the fire' is not a rhetorical flourish. In other Arabian travellers' tales, Sindbad and his real-life precursors always describe the people they meet on the way. In his Second Voyage Sindbad is horrified when he is left behind by his shipmates mainly because there is *no one there*. Someone — presumably in the Middle East and long ago — noticed that there is only one animal which *blows on fire*, and in this strange new land, that particular creature is nowhere to be seen.

Burton expands on this in a footnote, stating that 'not a blower of the fire' was a popular Arabic phrase to express 'utter desolation'. Desolation in Burton's time did not mean misery and destruction so much as the absence of human company. By the eleventh century, only one large temperate landmass remained in the world where there were no human inhabitants, no blowers on fire, and where a castaway would be in utter desolation, and that was the country named Aotearoa by early Tahitian visitors and then New Zealand by Europeans.

The sweet-smelling trees, the birdsong, the clear streams — these also fit the descriptions of other early arrivals from Eurasia. Joseph Banks, for example, the botanist on Cook's ship *Endeavour*, was famously woken in his cabin one morning by the sounds from a shoreline forest: 'This morn I was awakd by the singing of birds ashore from where we are distant not a quarter of a mile, the numbers of them were certainly very great, their voices were certainly the most melodious wild musick I have ever heard almost imitating small bells but with the most tuneable silver sound imaginable to which maybe the distance was no small addition.'[6]

That was written in 1770. By then, New Zealand had been occupied for about 500 years by Polynesians who had brought dogs with them, and rats: the native birdlife was already greatly diminished. If there really were Muslim visitors in the tenth or eleventh century, the singing would have been louder still, although where an eighteenth-century English botanist heard 'melodious wild musick', the Muslims, as described by Burton (an atheist fascinated by religion), heard something different: 'The merchants and sailors walked about enjoying the shade of the trees and the song of the birds, that chanted the praises of the One, the Victorious, and marvelling at the works of the Omnipotent King.'

But was such a journey by Sindbad or a man from the Maghreb or anywhere else in the Islamic world remotely possible in the tenth or eleventh centuries? Professor Bivar was probably right when he suggested that New Zealand historians were generally sceptical, yet no one doubts the fact that by 1000 CE other people who also originated in Asia had been ranging far and wide over the Pacific for at least 1500 years.

And now that the presence of a giant eagle in Aotearoa has been established beyond doubt, references in the records left by those early Pacific navigators to a 'bird-fiend' living in a strange land which they named Hiti Marama take on a distinct historical significance.

Chapter 12

Long before Māori reached New Zealand, their ancestors had come out of Southeast Asia and settled in the islands of the tropical Pacific. From there, over many centuries, different navigator-heroes made voyages in all directions, evidently reaching the coast of South America, as well as sighting icebergs in the Southern Ocean on at least one occasion. At certain times, according to the contradictory though highly formulaic accounts of these voyages, a 'demon bird' attacks the explorers near an enchanted land named Hiti Marama, ruled by Puna, the goblin king.

Here is a Tahitian version of the story, which involves an explorer named Rata: 'Rata set out again to seek and kill other monsters lurking abroad on land and sea. One day the sun became darkened as with a great cloud and there came with large outspread wings an immense, black bird-fiend with fierce glance and wild screech, and the men all exclaimed

"Ua pohe tatou!" (We are lost!) and rose with their spears for the deadly struggle. But the priest exclaimed:

'"This is the demon Matutu-ta'o-ta'o of the ogre-king Puna, of Hiti-Marama. He will surely die at the hands of the warriors of Tahiti."

'Just then the bird soared high and, with its hooked beak open and talons outstretched, it descended to attack Rata but as it swept on him he darted his spear into its throat. The spears of the other men soon broke its wings, and pierced it through the heart.'[7]

This tale was recorded by missionaries in Tahiti in the nineteenth century and Rata is depicted as a Tahitian hero. But the cycle of Rata stories is one of the most ancient in Polynesia, much older than settlement of Tahiti. Rata was not a single individual. There are many Ratas, or Latas, or Rakas moving along the horizon of Polynesian history. If some great navigator emerged and set off and found new islands, he was given the name of a shadowy predecessor who had done the same thing perhaps 500 or 1000 years before.

The essence of Polynesian history *was* movement — embarkation from a previous home known as Hawaiki. And there were many Hawaikis — a line of islands like stepping-stones stretches from central Polynesia far back to the west and to the Asian mainland itself. Some of the names are still on the maps — Savai'i (in Sāmoa), Sawai (in Indonesia), possibly Java itself, and Taiwan. The word 'Hawaiki' probably contains the sense of 'water' and 'distance' — in other words 'overseas' — and could therefore be bestowed on both the new land — Hawai'i is an obvious example — and the old one.

The people of the Marquesas can recall and name

seventeen of these stepping stones. DNA studies and
linguistics prove that one early and certain Hawaiki was the
island of Taiwan. The ancestors of the indigenous Taiwanese
came from the Asian mainland 8000 years ago. A nineteenth-
century Māori source offers this: 'Hawaiki Nui [Great Hawaiki]
was a mainland with vast plains on the side towards the sea
and a high range of snowy mountains; through the country
ran the river Tohinga.'[8] This description could apply to many
places, including Taiwan, but if the continental mainland is
meant, it may be the easternmost ranges of the Himalayas
which here rise into view . . .

The progress down through Southeast Asia and out across
the Pacific was not smooth or even. There were long delays, at
times lasting 1000 years. In 1952 two American archaeologists
excavating a site on a peninsula on Grande Terre island in
New Caledonia, far out in the Pacific, found a number of
reddish-brown potsherds patterned with 'dentate' markings, as
if made by the teeth of a comb. This was to become known
as Lapita ware. The name was the result of a misunderstanding
between the Americans and the indigenous people, the Kanaks.
The conversation went something like this:

'What's the name of this place?'

'Why? Are you going to dig a hole?'

In the local Kanak dialect the verb 'to dig a hole' is xapeta'a.
The archaeologists took this as the answer to their question,
and the word was then conferred not only on the fragments
of baked clay they found a few feet down in the sandy soil,
but then on a whole culture which had once stretched from
Southeast Asia out into the Pacific. Similar fragments had
been found in different parts of that expanse, in Sulawesi in

Indonesia, on a Melanesian island named Watom, and far to the east, in the ocean kingdom of Tonga, but it was not until 1952 that the Americans saw the pattern, literally — the same dentate markings — in all those places and put the pieces together. They were made by people of a single culture.

That was one breakthrough. The other was the radiocarbon revolution. In the 1950s this method of dating material had just been invented. Some of the fragments found at 'Lapita' were sent to Michigan for radiocarbon dating and the oldest sample was found to be 3000 years old. The implications of this were huge: out of sight, far away from the civilisations of the Mediterranean, the Middle East, India or China, a brilliant technological advance had taken place. Human beings had found out how to cross the open-ocean barrier.

The history of humankind runs (at present) like this: 100,000 years ago *Homo sapiens* came out of Africa. Wandering a few miles a year, small bands split up and went in three directions — north into Europe, north-east into Asia, and south and east along the shores towards India and China and into the Sahul, the ancient continent which later became Papua and Australia. There, people halted, unable to proceed further. They were the ancestors of the Melanesians who still live there.

The journey so far had been by foot, or on drift-rafts or canoes which could reach nearby islands. *Intervisibility* is the term used. Humans were able to sail from one island to another if the second could be seen in the distance, or if it became visible at a point halfway or just over halfway between the two. The open ocean, however, where there was no land for hundreds of miles, was more or less impassable.

At the end of the chain of islands now named the Solomons, off the coast of Papua, there is an eastward gap of deep ocean 525 kilometres wide. No doubt during humankind's 25,000-year-long pause there on the brink of the Pacific, small canoes and rafts were swept out from time to time and some may even have made their way home again, but the distance and the difficulty were such that no deliberate migration was undertaken.

Then a new set of people arrived, the ancestors of the Polynesians. They halted there too, for at least a millennium, during which time they fought, skirted around and to some degree intermarried with the indigenous people. Then 3000 years ago, according to the record of Lapita shards, they moved on. The ocean gap was crossed. The way to the nearest oceanic islands had been opened, and beyond them to Vanuatu and New Caledonia, and then, rapidly, across wider and more dangerous ocean to Fiji, Sāmoa and Tonga. The Lapita people had sailed out into the Pacific further, faster and earlier than anyone had previously imagined. This was the information that came back from the University of Michigan.

Archaeologists descended on the region looking for more Lapita ware. Dozens of sites were examined across a 6500-kilometre arc. In 1976 another American, Roger Curtis Green, excavated one of the tiny Reef Islands, the first landfall across the ocean gap from the Solomons. It would be impossible even in the vastness of the Pacific to find a more remote and insignificant foothold for human beings, whether proto-Polynesian seafarers or modern archaeologists, than the Reef Islands in the Santa Cruz archipelago — dots of recrystallised coral rising a few metres above sea level. In satellite pictures they look like a spatter of paint, blue and white, flung by chance on a dark blue canvas.

Green was originally from New Jersey but his family moved to California, where he became interested in native American cultures. In the 1970s he was associate professor of anthropology at the University of Auckland. Our paths might have crossed there — I was at Auckland in the early seventies and anthropology was a fashionable subject; I had friends who spent the summer sieving middens on windswept headlands but I don't think I ever saw Roger Green. From the photographs, he is not someone you would forget. With his spade beard he looks at first like a Boer farmer, brawny neck and shoulders, and arms curved like the claw of an excavator. Closer examination of the pictures shows an intent and thoughtful man; you think of the gnomes and kobolds to whom the guardianship of buried treasure is entrusted in mediaeval stories.

In 1976, at a place named Nenumbo, on one of the Reef Islands, Green unearthed hundreds of Lapita sherds. Among them was one with an image. Clear, calm, confidently rendered, it was a human face.

The island in question was occupied by the original Lapita people for only about 50 years. Being the nearest point across the ocean from the Solomons, it is the oldest site that has been found in 'remote Oceania'. But whose face is looking out at us? Who is the man at Nenumbo? A simple answer would be no one at all, it is just a decorative motif, and certainly portraiture, the likeness of an individual, is a late development in art. But human faces were used before then to evoke spirit forces, notional ancestors, divine beings. Some of the forebears of the Polynesians came, as we saw, from Taiwan and they brought the art of pottery with them, specifically the 'red slip ware' found at Nenumbo and at Lapita. (A slip is the last coat applied before firing, to provide a coloured glaze.)

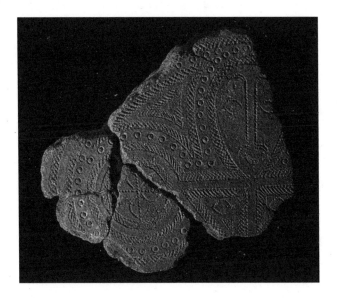

On their way down from Taiwan and through the Philippines, a journey lasting several thousand years, these potters kept their earthenware fairly plain. It was only in the islands north of Papua that faces begin to emerge among the dentate stamps. It is not, at first, entirely clear that the motifs *are* human faces. Some seem to have eyebrows and a nose and it has been suggested these do not represent human beings at all but the sea turtle. The face at Nenumbo, however, is unmistakable. It is a man. Similar faces look up from sherds found further east, in New Caledonia. But then, going even further into the Pacific, to Fiji and Tonga, they fade once more, the designs become more abstract, eventually there is no suggestion of a face and finally no decoration at all.

How do we explain this privileged, wide-eyed gaze that emerged from a coral pit on the Reef Islands, the first stopping-off point on humankind's first journey across the ocean? What happened at Nenumbo? It is impossible to overlook something rare in archaic art — the suggestion of a seraphic smile. Nenumbo Man's arms are stretched out. You might even say he has the world in his hands. Perhaps it is going too far to see in those features the face of an individual navigator, but they do suggest the confidence, the buoyant mood of people on an unprecedented career. For the first time, humans can sail out across the open ocean and, if they want to, sail back again. Perhaps, in the fragment dug up by Roger Green, we are looking into the eyes of the first Rata or Lata or Laka. (The main settlement of Santa Cruz and probably the oldest is, as it happens, still named Lata.)

After those first voyages, other Ratas emerged over the next 2000 years as the vastnesss of the Pacific was explored. 'Very deep is the well of the past,' said Thomas Mann in the prelude to his great, though currently unfashionable, novel *Joseph and his Brothers*. What Mann meant was that human history is extremely long and an old legend may relate not just to one event but to a series.

Before Noah's Flood, for instance, there must have been earlier great inundations in Mesopotamia — one every 5000 years would be a modest tally — and according to Mann's theory, the most recent both revives and obscures a vague memory of a previous one, a recognition, almost instinctual, that 'this has happened before' just as 'this is happening *now*' washes it away. The Rata in the Tahitian legend, in other words, would both renew and partly erase the memory of earlier Ratas who had explored the Pacific.

In all versions of the Rata story, however, there is one detail which remains unchanged. A tree is cut down to make a canoe but then, during the night, by enchantment, it is restored to the forest and has to be cut down a second time. Here, in a Tuamotuan version, Rata hides in the forest at night to see what is afoot: 'After a while he heard voices; then he saw a fairy whose name was Tava'a, who was followed by a number of others. Only parts of their bodies were visible — a foot, a nose, a leg, etc, and without visible hands. Tava'a was singing a powerful incantation:

> Fly together chips of my tree,
> Fly hither, fly hither,
> Pith of my tree. Stick fast together,
> Hold fast like glue,
> Stand upright, O tree![9]

In Rarotonga, 800 kilometres to the west, the same problem arose. With intense effort (Polynesians had no metal tools) a large tree was cut down but in the morning was back in place. Rata hides in the forest and waits. In this case, two gods named Atonga and Tongaiti-matarau arrive in the night 'like the rush of a mighty wind' and call upon the tree:

> Join together, come together,
> My beloved, my cherished ones.
> Rejoin your parents, O leaves.[10]

In the Samoan version, probably older still, it is Atonga's brothers who cut the tree down and Rata, the owner of the tree, who restores it with a powerful spell. Atonga, who is half spirit and half man, cuts it down again and makes a great canoe which is then sent on twelve voyages in all directions across the Pacific.

Hiding in the foliage of all these stories is a simple proposition: *two* trees were cut down. In short — the double-hull canoe has been invented. That seems to have been the achievement of the first Rata, or Lata, or Laka, and took place in the warm nursery-seas around the Solomons. Shelter for people and animals and for bulk food could now be built on a platform between two stable hulls, heavy sails could be put up, the horizons opened, and a wide-eyed gaze and something like a smile appears briefly on the slipware of the race . . .

It is only a theory and almost certainly faulty. In the space–time of the Pacific over three or four millennia there must have been movements and migrations we know nothing about, but as a working model this one may be useful, and, in the form of the story of Rata, is extremely persistent. In all versions, it is the final chapter of a saga which began generations before when Rata's forebears set out to sea and were never seen again. They vanished into the blue.

Demons and ogres must therefore have killed them. The demons in question were precisely the alarming creatures which occupy the thoughts of people on the edge of an unknown ocean — the shark, for example, the swordfish, the tridacna (giant clam), the giant octopus, and so on. Puna, their king, represents the unknown which takes on a hostile form in dreams. In all the versions, Rata, who now has new technology at his command and can come and go at will, sets out to look for his ancestors who disappeared over the years, and to avenge them by destroying the demons.

On many of these journeys Rata encounters an ogre named Matuku-tangotango. In some stories this Matuku is a shark or a giant lizard, in others a human being, the chief of a savage, pakiwhara ('naked') people, or those people themselves, or even the land where they lived. Possibly this is a reference to the Melanesians whom the Polynesians' ancestors encountered, and occasionally married, in or around Papua and the Solomons. Tangotango as an adjective means 'very dark'. As a verb, it has the sense of 'seize'. It also has human connotations — to slip through the dark to meet a lover. Rape is not suggested; it took two to tangotango.

Much later on, and far away in eastern Polynesia, the story changes again. Here the ogre Matuku-tangotango takes the form of a very dangerous bird, guarding an uncanny land named Hiti Marama. 'One day the sun darkened and there came with large outspread wings an immense, black bird-fiend with a fierce glance and wild screech . . . This is the demon Matutu-ta'ota'o of the ogre-king Puna.'

But where was Hiti Marama? Was it a real place, or a generic land-of-far-beyond where demons and ogres usually reside? Traditions differ in different parts of Polynesia. In one legend the land ruled by King Puna is placed north and west of Pitcairn Island, high in the tropics; in another, it has been lost — it 'sank forever into unknown depths'. There is much uncertainty. But the Pacific is vast. Odysseus was lost for ten years wandering the Mediterranean, about 2.6 million square kilometres of sea. The Pacific extends for 155 million. From one angle in space the planet is entirely blue.

Scattered across this dome of ocean, different groups of Polynesians might be isolated for generations and it would not be surprising if the records, transmitted orally, changed as they were passed down in separate places. Hiti Marama, in other words, wandered about, yet there are one or two persistent details which suggest the storytellers originally had a real place in mind. The Tuamotu legend (the Tuamotu islands are east of Tahiti) states that Puna, the king of the demons, is weak when *the cold south wind blows.* The same detail is found in the Hawaiian version. Hawai'i is thousands of kilometres from the Tuamotuans, and there is a rule of thumb which applies to oral traditions: the further apart the same story is heard, the older it must be. Hawai'i is north of the equator, and there the south wind is not cold. This detail, a *cold south wind*, suggests the demon king ruled a land well to the south of the equator.

There is another notable feature of Hiti Marama which points to a definite location. In the Tahitian version of the tale, Rata and his crew succeed in killing the demon-bird and then set out to find and punish Puna himself and thus they 'arrived at that wonderful land. It had a high embankment covered with dense foliage and in the background a single cone-shaped mountain which constantly caught the passing clouds, and from whose base gushed forth perennial springs of cool, clear water, irrigating the plains below.'[11] In the Tuamotuan version, Hiti Marama contains the same scenery: 'In the centre of the land was one solitary cone-shaped mountain which was white with the blossoms of the 'a'eho cane.'

The first very high mountain visible to sea voyagers arriving from the north is Taranaki, or Egmont as it was named by Cook. It must have been an extraordinary sight to Polynesians coming from the equatorial zone. It was extraordinary enough for the first Europeans arriving in the eighteenth century. Here is Joseph Banks again, on board Cook's ship *Endeavour*, on 13 January 1770, occasionally catching sight of the peak: 'This morn soon after day break we had a momentary view of our great hill the top of which was thick coverd with snow . . . How high it may be I do not take upon me to judge, but it is certainly the noblest hill I have ever seen . . . At sun set the top appeard again for a few minutes but the whole day it was covered with clouds.'[12]

Cook himself, the same day, wrote: 'At 5 am saw for a few Minutes the Top of the peaked Mountain above the Clowds . . . It is of a prodigious height and its top is cover'd with everlasting snow . . . [W]hat makes it more conspicuous is, its being situated near the Sea, and a flat Country in its neighbourhood . . . cloathed with Wood and Verdure.'[13]

The Europeans knew snow when they saw it. To Polynesians, who had spent many generations in the tropics, the white cloak covering a mountain in the distance must have been wholly mysterious. The blue-white blossom of a'aeho (sugar cane, a plant they had brought with them from South-east Asia) was perhaps an explanation.[14] When Māori finally did come to live in New Zealand they knew that snow was not the blossom of the sugar cane plant, but they still had no word for it and called it huka, which is the name for sea foam.

The Rata fables of course long precede the settlement of New Zealand and these Tuamotuan and Tahitian versions which report a 'black bird-fiend' in an enchanted land named Hiti Marama may therefore be the first historical reference we have to *Harpagornis*, and perhaps even the first name ever given to the land later called Aotearoa, and later still New Zealand.[15] Hiti means edge or border and marama means the moon, and in some translations Puna's kingdom is given the poetic if puzzling name 'Land of the Moon's Borders'. As an adjective, however, marama means clear, light, rational, easy to understand. The islands of New Zealand with their tall white peaks, weirdly long summer days and long winter nights, and the formidable birds — the boom of the moa alone would have been audible for miles out to sea — must have seemed to people coming from the tropical Pacific to stand at the very edge not only of the known world but also of all rational experience.

This is slight material on which to base the location of a large country but there is more evidence linking Hiti Marama to New Zealand. Several Māori legends collected in the nineteenth century recall a period before human settlement when the only inhabitants of the country were the kāhui tipua — a flock of goblins and ogres.

According to the accounts, these goblins lived in the North Island but were so quarrelsome that their king sent some of them into exile in the south. The worst-behaved are listed in the stories: Kōpūwai, a dog-headed monster, who ended up in a cave near the Mataau (Clutha) River; Ngārara Huarau, a part-lizard, part-man who was sent to Mohua (Golden Bay); and finally Pouākai, the eagle, who was exiled to Mount Tāwera, where he reappears in the later legend. Unfortunately, the king is not named in the Māori accounts so that identification of these ogres with the demons of the Hiti Marama legend is not completely certain. But there are later developments in the legends of Rata which bring them very close.

In one Māori version, Rata's grandfather is killed not by one but two demons, Matuku-tangotango and Pou-a-hao-kai. Rata sets out to avenge him. There is the usual preliminary in the forest — he fells a tree which springs back into place overnight — but eventually he sails away with his men to find the land of the demons. 'When they had got far out on the ocean, Rata said to his army: "If Pou-a-hao-kai should come out to make war on us, and if he should call out 'Little heads, little heads!' I will cry out 'Display the big head!'" On the beach, they were so numerous they covered the sand, and Pou-a-hao-kai opened his mouth in vain — he was unable to call out; so Rata and his men escaped destruction by that god.'[16]

Both demons are then killed: Pou-a-hao-kai is fed hot stones, while Matuku-tangotango, lured from a cave by the prospect of eating Rata alive, is trapped by men hidden behind woven fences, then speared and his wings broken. Here the story converges so closely with the legends about the Pouākai sent to live on Mount Tāwera, that it is plain that Pouākai and Pou-a-hao-kai are the same creature and that the Matuku-tangotango is associated with both. Hiti Marama, in other words, where earlier Rata figures went to avenge their ancestors, now has a distinct connection, through the eagle named Pouākai, to the new land which Māori themselves have now settled.[17]

There may be some archaeological evidence that this pairing of the demons was also known in the wider Polynesian world.

In 1920 a strange, archaic carving was found when a swamp was drained near Kaitāia in the far north of New Zealand. It is described as a lintel or roof-comb or a threshold ornament and shows a small human figure with two creatures, birds or lizards, one on each side. Now known to Te Rarawa as Tāngonge Waharoa, it is quite unlike any later Māori carving.

The central figure, however, has very close relatives in the sculpture of Tahiti and the Austral Islands, south of Tahiti, but this sculpture is made of wood of the tōtara, a tree which grows only in New Zealand, so it hasn't come from abroad. It must be the work of an early visitor or settler who brought with him the sculptural style of eastern Polynesia and, presumably, legends from the same place.

So who is the little figure in the middle? Māori in Kaitāia today will say only that he is an ancestor whose identity is now forgotten. It is very likely that whoever made the sculpture was indeed one of their ancestors, but what is his subject matter? And who or what are the two demons carving the air behind them in elegant chevrons? Could the sculpture be read as a depiction of the goblin king Puna and his servants Matuku-tangotango and Pou-a-hao-kai, which guard the legendary country of Hiti Marama, where settlers from eastern Polynesia, including the carver himself, now found themselves living? If that is the case, there is an element of genius in the work. There are limits to the powers of sculpture. You cannot, for instance, carve a *sound*. Did this artist working centuries ago somewhere near modern Kaitāia find a way, through those lethal chevrons, to suggest the fearful sound of fast-approaching wingbeats?

In another Māori story about the demon-bird, the hero is not named Rata but Pungarehu, who lives in Hawaiki (in this case probably Tahiti). He and a companion are blown out to sea in a storm and arrive on an unknown shore. They meet a primitive people, the Nuku-mai-tore, who live in trees and do not know how to make fire and cook food. One of the Nuku-mai-tore warns the visitors: 'If any of our half-witted people come to meet and dance to us, and you laugh at them, they will kill you.'

That night, the dancers come to entertain the strangers. In their hands they hold primitive weapons made of flint or of sharks' teeth lashed to a wooden handle. As they dance, they sing:

> Now you laugh,
> Now you don't,
> Now you laugh,
> Now you don't.

Sensibly, Pungarehu and his companion do not laugh. Instead, they light a fire and cook a meal of whale meat.

'When the fumes of the smoke got into the nostrils of the people they exclaimed:

"Whispering ghosts of the west,

Who brought you here

To our land?

Stand up and depart.

Whispering ghosts of the west,

Who brought you here

To our land?

Stand up and depart."

But then the Nuku-mai-tore eat some of the roasted meat and are won over. Cooked food is delicious! 'They then said to Pungarehu, "There is one thing which is an evil to us. It is Pouākai, a bird which eats man."'[18]

Pungarehu then builds a trap in the form of a house with a window as the only opening and kills the terrible bird when it flies down. It is a story of civilising influence — fire, cooking, ridding the land of ogres — but here the demon Matuku-tangotango has disappeared, leaving only the Pouākai,[19] and soon the wild Nuku-mai-tore also depart from view, being mentioned only occasionally in later stories about the many fairy folk and spirits with whom Māori believed they shared their new homeland — the Patupaiarehe, for instance, who were never seen but only heard laughing and retreating further into the forest as you approached; the Tūrehu, who were known to have affairs with human women, and taught them the art of weaving; the Awaru, who were only ever heard singing out to sea; their near relations, the Irewaru, heard only at night along the coasts; the Tutuamaio, seen on beaches by day but always far ahead and vanishing as you came near; the Pakepakehā who were heard singing as they rode on pieces of driftwood down rivers in flood, and who had their own race of fairy folk to contend with, the Porotai, half wood and half stone, who of course were never seen or heard at all by ordinary people, existing as they did at not one but two angles from human reality.[20]

It was into this select society that Pouākai or Te Hōkioi also departed, as the eagle became rare and evidently no longer represented a threat. Te Hōkioi started to move up the ladder socially, becoming a descendant of the brightest star in the sky, Rehua (possibly Sirius or Antares), the symbol of midsummer, and also of the eye 'which never winks' of a young warrior. He then became an intermediary with the gods, living with them in the 'spacious temple called holiness in heaven', as in this kite-flying chant:

> Go up, go up,
> To this side of the wind,
> The door is open
> The channel is open,
> To the highest heaven,
> To the seventh heaven,
> To the eighth heaven,
> The world is made one with space,
> Where is the sacredness?
> In the tranquil temple called
> 'Holiness in heaven',
> Climb now to your ancestor,
> The Hōkioi.[21]

Finally, Te Hōkioi is not merely a messenger to the gods — he is almost a god himself:

A Hokioi on high, a Hokioi on high, *hu*!

Dwelling afar in celestial space,

Sleeping-companion of Whaitiri-Matakataka[22]

Whaitiri-Matakataka was the goddess of thunder, a terrifying figment of the imagination — hostile, striding the sky, extremely dangerous — who dwelt *far above, and hard by the Cloud House.*[23] The Cloud House was not so much a place in Māori cosmogony as a poeticism, although one based on natural observation: since at times clouds are scattered across the sky and at other times none can be seen, it was logical to assume they had a gathering place. This was the Cloud House, Te Ahoaho o Tukapua, which on occasion might even come into view, as a thundercloud, ominously tall, hard-edged, apparently solid like stone.

Here the Rata legend has come full circle. We see a pillar of cumulus begin to flicker, and hear it rumble, and there is a dark shape on the wing nearby: the bird-fiend which guarded Hiti Marama is now bed-mate of the thunder goddess herself, whose own descendant, Rata, was the first to set out over the ocean to avenge those of his forebears who had sailed away and were never seen again.

Chapter 13

About 1500 years after Polynesians first sailed out into the Pacific, a Chinese monk named Fa-Hsien who had just spent six years in India departed for his own country. Fa-Hsien had walked to India from China, crossing deserts and mountain ranges and taking several years to do so. Now he was going home by sea. This was in the year 413 CE. His ship left the city of Tamralipta, then the chief port of the Gupta empire, and sailed down the coast to Ceylon. There Fa-Hsien took passage on a larger ship with over 200 people aboard and they set out across the open sea for Java. Terror ensued.

'The Great Ocean spreads out in a boundless expanse,' Fa-Hsien wrote. 'There is no knowing east or west. Only by observing the sun, moon and stars was it possible to go forward. If the weather was dark or rainy the ship went as she was carried by the wind, without any definite course. In the darkness of night only the great waves were to be seen, breaking on one another, emitting a brightness like that of fire, with huge turtles and other monsters of the deep all about. The merchants were full of terror, not knowing where they were going. The sea was deep and bottomless, and there was no place where they could let down a stone and stop . . .'[24]

Fa-Hsien's ship, in fact, did almost founder. It sprang a leak, the merchants duly panicked and tried to transfer to a smaller vessel in tow, but the men aboard that vessel cut the rope and drifted away. The merchants then began to throw their goods overboard to lighten the load. Fa-Hsien joined in, hurling his pitcher and wash basin into the sea, hoping this would look good enough and the merchants would not remember all the books and sacred images he had carried on board.

The whole purpose of his journey to India had been to track down certain Buddhist scriptures which could not be found in China. After crossing north and central India he had reached the city of Pataliputra whose walls and gates, being on a scale and of a beauty beyond anything that 'human hands of this world could accomplish', must have been constructed, he thought, by spirits. There he found what he was looking for: two versions of the rules of monastic discipline, the *Mahasanghika* and the *Sarvastivada*, and as well as that the *Samyukthabi-dharma-hridaya*, containing detailed classifications of doctrine.

Above all, Fa-Hsien admired order and moderation. He was in India in its golden age, under the Gupta kings. '*This* should be named the Middle Kingdom,' he wrote, scandalising all future generations of Chinese. 'In it cold and heat are finely tempered and there is neither hoarfrost nor snow . . . the people are numerous and happy . . . the king governs without decapitation or corporal punishments. Criminals are merely fined, lightly or heavily according to the circumstances. Even in cases of repeated attempts at wicked rebellion, they only have their right hand cut off . . . Throughout the whole country the people do not kill any living creature, nor drink intoxicating liquor nor eat onions.'

Now he was lost at sea in an endless tempest, not knowing east or west, and if the merchants didn't throw overboard the texts he had spent five years translating from Sanskrit, the waves might very well tower over the ship and take them anyway, and him with them, and if the storm subsided there were still pirates everywhere 'to meet with whom is speedy death', and if the ship came upon 'any hidden rock' then there was no escape at all.

On his walk from China to India, Fa-Hsien had encountered sandstorms, insurrections, terrifying precipices and certain venomous dragons which 'when provoked, spit forth poisonous winds, showers of snow and storms of sand and gravel'. All those seemed slight impediments compared to the horror of travel across the ocean.

After ten days, in fact, the storm abated, the sky cleared, they knew east from west again and continued to Java, where Fa-Hsien then embarked on a third ship, this one bound for southern China. But the third leg of the journey was worse than the second. They were now entering the typhoon zone. 'In this sea is often beheld a white Cloud which at once spreads over a ship and lets down a long, thin Tongue or Spout quite to the Surface of the water,' another early traveller wrote, 'which it disturbs just after the Manner of a Whirl-wind and if a Vessel happens to be in the way of this Whirl-pool she is immediately swallowed up thereby ... All these Seas are subject to great Commotions excited by the Winds which make them boil up like Water over a fire. Then it is that the Surf dashes ships against the Islands and breaks them to pieces with unspeakable Violence and then also is it that Fish, of all sizes, are thrown dead ashore upon the Rocks, like an Arrow from a Bow.'[25]

The journey from Java to Guangzhou in south China usually took about 60 days. At first, all went well, Fa-Hsien wrote, but one night after a month at sea 'when the night-drum sounded the second watch, they encountered a black wind and tempestuous rain which threw the merchants and passengers into consternation ... After day-break, the Brahmans deliberated together and said "It is having this *Sramana* [a monk, literally 'a seeker after truth' — namely, Fa-Hsien] on board which has occasioned our misfortune and brought us to this great and bitter suffering. Let us put him ashore on some island-shore."'

That was a prospect almost worse than being drowned. The islanders, the sea-peoples of the Indian Ocean and the China Seas, were terrifying. In Taiwan 'the people go naked and are in a state of primitive savagery like beasts' wrote the Chinese author of *A Description of Barbarian Peoples.* In the Philippines, 'their eyes are yellow and round, they have curly hair and their teeth show. They nest in tree-tops. Sometimes parties of three or five lurk in the jungle and shoot arrows at passers-by unseen. If thrown a porcelain bowl, they will stoop and pick it up and go away leaping and shouting for joy.'[26]

The coasts of Borneo were more dangerous still: 'When

traders are driven to this country, these savages assemble in large numbers and having caught the shipwrecked, they roast them over a fire with large bamboo pincers and eat them. They use human skulls as vessels for drinking and eating.' Most feared of all were the people of the Andaman Islands. 'The natives are as black as lacquer and eat men alive so that sailors do not dare anchor on the coast,' one Chinese source said. Arabs took the same view of the Andamanese: 'Their Complexion is black; their hair Frizled; their Countenance and Eyes frightful; their Feet are very large and almost a Cubit in length; and they go quite naked. They have no Embarkations; if they had they would devour all Passengers they could lay Hands on.'

Fa-Hsien was saved from a castaway's fate by an unnamed 'patron' aboard the ship, who told the Indian merchants that if the bishku — the monk — was put ashore, they would have to put him off as well, or kill him, since he would certainly report them to the king of China — if they ever got there. The Brahmans relented. The ship sailed on, but still no one knew where they were. 'The sky continued dark and gloomy and the sailing-masters looked at one another and made mistakes.'

More than 70 days had passed since leaving Java. They were now running short of food and water. They had clearly missed the southern port of Guangzhou. Had they missed China altogether? Here was another dread, worse still than the others — to sail on out into the Great Encircling Ocean, from which no one ever returned. There was a good reason for this. If you sailed far enough to the south-east, as everyone knew, the sea began to *slope*. This was a very old belief which derived from the idea that there was a hole or drain, the wei-lu, in the sea-floor. The wei-lu first appeared as a minor detail in a Chinese folk story. Long ago, in the era of the mythical Xia dynasty, a red-haired ogre named Gong Gong fought and lost a battle against the god of fire. Gong Gong was so ashamed that he smashed his head against one of the pillars holding up the sky. This caused the sky to tilt to the north-west. As a consequence, the major rivers of China began to flow towards the east and south-east, as they still do. Since the ocean did not overflow, it was logical to assume that there was a drain, and that the drain was somewhere in the same direction, to the south and east. This was the wei-lu.

Above the drain, naturally, a whirlpool would form on a gigantic scale. In short, the water of the ocean began to circle and speed up and tilt. Any ship sailing too far south and east would be caught in this downward spiral and irrevocably lost. This, in turn, explained why so few of the ships swept east into the ocean by typhoons were ever seen again. The existence of the wei-lu was firmly believed for many centuries in China and in the other maritime civilisations. In 1178 a Chinese official, Chou K'u-fei, described the situation succinctly. 'To the east of Java is the Great Eastern Ocean-Sea where the surface of waters begin to go downwards; there is the kingdom of women. Still further east is the place where the wei-lu drains into the world from which men do not return.'

A tenth-century Persian writer, a ship's captain known as Buzurg ibn Shahriyar, gave more details in *The Book of the Marvels of India*: 'A ship set out from India, passed Malaya and then drew near the confines of China, and had already caught sight of some mountainous eminence when a sudden and frightful wind sprang up, blowing against the vessel's course, so violently there was no withstanding it, while the fury of the waves put steering out of the question. The wind drove them towards Canopus. Now whoever, in those seas, is blown so far that Canopus stands overhead [that is, south of the Equator] let that man abandon all hope of return. He is hurried along upon a mass of water rushing to the south and as the ship proceeds the waves are heaped up behind him — on one side, that is to say, and on the other the flood declines before him.

'Thus, whatever may be the wind, all ways of escape are shut and the current draws him down across the immensity of the ocean. And when the ship's company saw that they were rushing towards Canopus, and night had come on, and they beheld a thick darkness all around, they despaired of their lives . . . and they bade one another goodbye, and severally each man invoked the power of the deity he served, for there were among them men of China, India, Persia, and from the isles, and one man from Cádiz, in Spain, for there happened to be on the ship a Musulman, a native of Cádiz, who had slipped aboard and stowed away and hid. In the storm and fear, he came forth from his hiding place.

'"Who are you?"

'"A stowaway."

'"But how did you live?"

'"On a plate of rice with butter in it, that one of your sailors set down near my hiding place every day, and a saucer of water too, for the guardian angel of the ship."'

Luckily, at least for the man of Cádiz, the ship reached the coast of the kingdom of women and he was saved, although the kingdom of women was almost as dangerous as the sloping waters of wei-lu, since most sailors who landed there soon died of sexual exhaustion. The man of Cádiz survived the excitements and even sailed back and reported his story, confirming beyond doubt the existence of both the kingdom of women and the wei-lu.

To avoid a similar fate, the sailing-masters of Fa-Hsien's ship, lost at sea in the fifth century, now turned north-west. They sailed for twelve days, then they sighted land and went ashore. 'Not seeing, however, any inhabitants nor any traces of them, they did not know whereabouts they were.' Then they saw certain vegetables, the lei and the kwoh, growing nearby and they 'knew indeed it was the land of the Han'.

They had arrived in Shandong, 1900 kilometres north of their intended destination, but until they saw the two familiar (though now unidentified) vegetables, they were not sure they were even in China. 'To reach China and not perish . . . that in itself was regarded as a considerable feat,' wrote the author of *The Marvels of India*, 'but to come back again, safe and sound, was a thing unheard of. I have heard that no one apart from one man has made two journeys, coming and going, entirely without mischance.'

This then was travel on the oceanic route between India and China in the fifth century, about 1500 years since a Rata or Lata or Laka set out from the Solomon Islands. There is some debate about when travel out of sight of the coasts actually began in the Indian ocean. Claims of its antiquity are attributed to Buddha himself: 'Long ago ocean-going merchants used to plunge forth upon the sea on board a ship taking with them a shore-sighting bird and setting it free. And it would go to the east and to the south and the west and the north and the intermediate points and rise aloft. If on the horizon it caught sight of land thither it would go. But if not, then it would come back to the ship again.'[27]

This has been taken as evidence that when Buddha was alive, in about 400 BCE, deep-water sailing was routine, although the text rather suggests the opposite. Birds were taken on board not in order to sail out of sight of land but in order not to. If by chance you were blown far out to sea, land-dwelling birds kept in cages on the ship could be set free and, flying up, would circle the mast and then go off in the direction of safety. The technique was ancient. Noah, according to the Hebrew account, carried ravens and doves on the Ark and put them to the task. The same detail is found in the Greek tale of the Flood and in the Babylonian epic of Gilgamesh written down about 2000 BCE.

It was not until about 100 BCE that we can be sure that Arab traders had learned to 'catch the monsoon' and sail from Somalia straight out across the ocean to India, far from the sight of land for the whole journey. Oceanic trade routes further east, from India to Java, and then on to China, were established in the next 200 years. The trade was very dangerous. *To reach China and not perish . . . was a considerable feat.* But the dangers added to the rarity of the goods, sent up the prices and made the trade irresistible.

By the time Fa-Hsien arrived in India, the Gupta empire, with its rich cities lining the banks of the Ganges for 1600 kilometres inland and its chief port, Tamralipta, famous for the wit of its inhabitants and the illuminations of their houses, had turned its full attention to the 'gold countries' over the sea to the east.

The great literary achievement of the era, *The Romance of the Aerial Spirits*, is filled with the sound of breaking waves: 'The merchant Sanmudrasura went by sea to Surnvarnadvipa. A terrible cloud arose and agitated the deep . . . The ship was struck by a sea-monster and split asunder. The merchant, girding up his loins, plunged into the sea. Then he rode a corpse to safety and found in its loincloth a necklace of inestimable value.

'Then he went to a city called Kalasapura where he was seen with the necklace and accused of theft. At that moment a kite saw it glittering and swooping down from heaven he carried off the necklace and disappeared. The king ordered the man be put to death and he, in great grief, invoked the protection of Siva, and then a voice was heard from heaven "Do not put this man to death. He is an innocent man." The king heard this and let the merchant go. Again he set forth and crossed the terrible ocean . . .'

This sounds so like the tales of Sindbad we can safely assume a connection, although *The Romance* was written at least 500 years before the Sindbad cycle. First related by Shiva to his wife, the Daughter of the Mountain, it eventually reached the ears of a human being, a sage named Gunadhya who decided to write the stories down. Gunadhya's problem was that, in order to prevent certain aerial spirits from stealing the tales, he had to hide in the forest. There, lacking ink, he used his own blood to write them down.

He also wrote the stories in an obscure tongue — the 'trolls' language'. This suggests an indigenous language was used, or perhaps a 'dead' literary language — in any case not classical Sanskrit — and perhaps points to a pre-Aryan source for some of the stories. The Gupta king was disgusted by the blood and the trolls' language and rejected the book. Mortified, Gunadhya went back to the forest and burnt his work on a hilltop, reading page after page to the birds and beasts before committing the pages to the flames.

The creatures were so entranced by the stories they forgot to eat and also forgot to provide Gunadhya with food. Literature and privation have a long history. The Gupta king, however, then realised his error, hurried to the forest and saved the last section, which is all that has come down to us today but which, at 66,000 lines, is still twice as long as all of Homer.

The text saved by the king has not survived. *The Romance* exists in several later recensions. One writer, Somadeva, translated it into Sanskrit in the twelfth century, and since he thought it contained all the stories ever told, just as the ocean contains the flow of all the rivers, he divided the work into 124 chapters called tarangas — 'waves' or 'billows' — and the book was then renamed *The Ocean of the Rivers of Story*. Filled with tales of shipwreck and uncanny lands, the book had become a kind of ocean itself, like the one which provided much of its material.

The eastward-gazing Gupta civilisation was highly mercantile but it was not only traders who sailed to the 'gold countries'. With them travelled the pantheon of Hindu gods and goddesses, Buddhist spirits and the semi-divine beasts and guardian demons of both Indian religions. The ruins of Angkor Wat in Cambodia and Borobudur in Indonesia show the scale and grandeur of this diffusion. The Hindu eagle, for instance, Garuda, which is still seen guarding the palaces and on the tailfins of airlines across Southeast Asia, began life as a battle emblem for Aryan tribes fighting their way down through the mountains into India, rather as the eagle of Zeus — probably a relation — is first seen in the war against the old pre-Olympic gods of Greece. The later career of Zeus's eagle is well known — he was an emblem of Roman Jupiter and the Roman legions and was adopted by later European royal houses; he appears on Napoleon's battle standards, on the pennants of German staff cars in the Second World War, and has reappeared on the flag of a bellicose Russia.

In India, Garuda evolved rather differently. Born, according to the epic *Mahabarata*, in a starburst 'enkindling all the points of the universe . . . increasing like a mountain of flames, appeasing his hunger by hawking for elephants as the kestrel hawks for the mouse', his home for the next thousand years was the Himavant — the Himalayas or the Pamir mountains — or on sacred Mount Meru, 84,000 yojanas (672,000 miles) high, standing beyond a river of gold in the frozen north.

During his early adventures in India, Garuda was the *chariot* of the god Vishnu, fighting the nagas or serpents, probably a reference to the indigenous peoples of the subcontinent, but by the tenth century Hinduism had triumphed and Garuda now appears in sophisticated parables about illusion, gender, reality. The sage Narada, for example, meets Vishnu and asks him for a glimpse of Maya, or Illusion. 'I, Narada, asked the Lord of the World: "What is the form of Maya? How is she? What is the form of her strength?"

'Vishnu said: "O Narada, if you want to see Maya, then come quickly and mount with me on Garuda: we will both go elsewhere and I will show you that Maya, invincible to those who have not conquered themselves . . ."

'Vishnu mounted on Garuda and gladly made me get up on his back with him. In a moment Garuda went, at his command, with the speed of wind and we saw beautiful forests, lovely lakes, rivers and towns, villages, huts of cultivators, towns close to the mountains, huts for cow-keepers in cowsheds, tanks, lakes beautified with lotuses, flocks of ewes, packs of wild boars and so on, till at last we came to a place close to Kanauj where I saw a beautiful tank where the lotus blossomed, the humming of bees ravished the mind, geese cackled, birds sang and the water itself, sweet as milk, defied the ocean.'

Vishnu tells Narada to bathe. Putting aside his lute and deerskin, Narada steps into the water, Vishnu vanishes and Narada emerges to find he has taken on a female form and has no memory of his former existence, lute or deerskin, the gods or even Lord Vishnu. He — she, that is — then meets a prince who naturally is passing on a chariot at that moment and who stops and questions her. She can tell him nothing. 'I do not know whose daughter I am, nor do I know quite certainly where are my mother and father. Someone placed me here by this tank and has gone away, whither I do not know.'

The prince marries her, she bears him twelve sons, many years pass. Her sons and daughters-in-law quarrel, another king invades with an army of chariots and elephants, her sons are all killed and then, surrounded by her dead children, she laments her sorrow-filled life.

A Brahmin priest appears and tells her this is all a delusion. He leads her to a tank to bathe. Stepping into the water,

Narada regains his memory and his male form, and there is Vishnu again, and the lute and deerskin, with the water droplets still on them from just a moment before . . .

This is a rich and more elaborate version of the Chinese fable in which the sage Zhuangzi fell asleep and dreamed he was a butterfly fluttering here and there, and then woke and could never be sure again whether he was a man who had dreamed he was a butterfly or a butterfly dreaming he was a man.

In this new Hindu world of cowherds and lotus ponds and leisure to think, Garuda himself changes appearance. The great eagle of the *Mahabarata* is gone. The oldest extant image of Garuda, on a lintel of the Buddhist temple of Sanchi, first century CE, shows a very large parrot with a head tuft and earrings. Over the next ten centuries he changes again and again — he is variously a plum-bird, a stork, the fish-eating Sifrid bird — and then he achieves his final Hindu form as a cherub with a man's head and arms, but with clawed feet, outspread wings, a necklace, long earrings and elaborate coiffure.

Strict priestly instructions on the finer points of his appearance were issued from time to time, generally contradicting each other:

'The nose should be like the beak of a parrot, the forepart of the foot like that of a goose, the face with fangs, the face as white as the complexion of the nails; he should have wings of a bird, the wings a mixture of five colours, his look terrifying, the crown on his head like the comb of the cock' (Manasara, c. 400 CE).

'Garuda should have the colour of emerald, the neck and legs of a kite, the eyes rounded, four arms, and a pair of golden wings of golden yellow lustre, and he should have a flabby belly' (Vishnudharmottara, c. 550 CE).

'The image should be golden from feet to knees, snow-white from knees to naval, scarlet from navel to neck, and black from neck to head, the eyes yellow, the beak blue, the look in the eyes terrific' (Silparatna, c. 1500 CE).

Meanwhile his habitat also changed. Mount Meru and the Himavant fade from view or in some cases move physically to the south and over the sea. The 'gold countries' in the east which had opened up to the Indian imagination must have seemed a more exotic and mystic address, more likely to be the home of the gods, than cold mountains to the north. Garuda is now found living on a mountain-top in Malaya, or 'over the innumerable billows of the sea' in a grove of trees in Java.

The same drift southward is in the *Jatakas*, a collection of folk tales woven over many centuries around the teaching and life of Buddha. 'Now at that time a *garula* bird which dwelt in a silk-cotton tree in Himavant, in a region of the great ocean, swept up the water with the wind of its wings and swooped on the land of the Naga region, seized a Naga king by the head,' one of the *Jatakas* tells us.[28] Or the mountains of the Himavant are dispensed with altogether and the 'young garudas live in the forests of mighty silk-cotton trees, far away over innumerable crests of the southern deep'.

In another *Jataka*, Garuda abducts the queen of Varanasi. The king's minstrel is sent to find her. The minstrel hides in the plumage of Garuda and flies to the palace on Mount Meru, but Mount Meru now has a grove of simbal trees and is on an island 'across seven oceans'. In another version, the minstrel 'takes a ship going to the golden land' and is shipwrecked on Naga Island where Garuda is now the king. Naga Island is described in some detail. It is somewhere beyond Ceylon, and contains a goblin town peopled by she-goblins: 'When a ship is wrecked they adorn themselves and taking rice and gruel and with trains of slaves, and with children on their hips, they come to the shipwrecked merchants and offer them the gruel . . . Then they lead them back to the goblin city and bind them with chains and cast them into the house of torment.'

It is hard to imagine what gave rise to this alarming fantasy but it may be related to the Arab and Chinese legends of a land east of Java inhabited by women alone, which has been tentatively identified with Papua. In any case we are now in a new world — equatorial, oceanic and inhabited by strange and dangerous peoples.

At some point in his history, Garuda also flew west and entered into Persian mythology, where he became known as the Roc, or Rukh, or Rukhkh (the Persian word rukh is linked to 'chariot').[29] When the time came for the Arabian and Persian zoological works to be written, it was to the fundamentally Hindu Garuda that the writers turned when giving accounts of a giant eagle which lived somewhere over the 'China Seas'. The Rukh by then had also crossbred or become interchangeable with the ancient Persian Simurgh, the Anqa of Arabia, and the griffin or lion-eagle which seems to have originated further west still, in Crete and Greece.

In his *Marvels of Creation and Strange Things Existing*, the Persian writer Zakariya al-Qazwini not only repeats the legend of the Anqa exiled to the southern seas but also almost gives us a sighting: 'Anqa is greatest of the birds in form and the largest in body. It hawks for elephants as a kestrel takes a mouse. In ancient times it preyed on people and carried off a bride adorned, and . . . Allah removed it to certain islands of the Ocean beyond the Equator, where it lives on an island which no man has reached. When it flies there is heard from its feathers a sound like the approach of a flood or the noise of trees in a tempest of wind. Moreover, the following is related on the authority of certain traders: "We strayed from our course into the Great Encircling Ocean and we were in perplexity. And lo! We were overshadowed by a great darkness like a dark cloud. The sailors said 'That is the Anqa,' and we followed it until we had entered into that darkness. Then our tongues were loosened in prayers. And it did not cease from travelling with us until we had regained our course . . . Then it vanished from us.'"

Al-Qazwini wrote his *Marvels* about 1270 CE and he must have known the story about the man from the Maghreb, but his tale is different: there is no actual sighting of the bird, no egg, no attack, only a dark cloud which alarms the sailors. Yet two things have happened here. The presence of the Anqa (or Simurgh or Rukh) on an island below the equator is now assumed by the sailors to be a fact. Secondly, if you are lost in that region, it is now quite possible to 'regain your course'.

Almost exactly the same thing happened 100 years later, as recorded by the celebrated Arab traveller Ibn Battuta. Like the man from the Maghreb, Ibn Battuta sails from India to China and back again. By this time naval technology has improved. Chinese ships, for instance, have become huge. 'They are like houses,' wrote the annalist Chou K'u-fei. 'When the sails are spread, they are like great clouds in the sky. Their rudders are several tens of feet long. A single ship carries several hundred men. It has stored on board a year's supply of grain. There is no account taken of dead or living, no going back to the mainland when once they have entered on the dark blue sea. When on board the gong sounds the day, the animals drink gluttonly, guests and hosts alike forgetting their perils.'

Ibn Battuta himself describes a junk with a thousand crew — 600 sailors and 400 marines — large enough not only to withstand heavy weather but also to carry enough armed men to repel attacks from the dangerous islanders, the seafolk, the 'black slave devils' as the Chinese called them.

Ibn Battuta's own journey was on a smaller vessel, manned by Muslims, probably from Ceylon and Java. Towards the end of his life he wrote or dictated an account of his travels in a book with the resounding title *The Rihla*, or *A Gift to Those Who Contemplate the Wonders of Cities and the Marvels of Travelling*. 'When I arrived in al-Zaitun [in southern China] I found the junks about to sail for India. Among them was a junk belonging to al-Malik al-Zahir, the lord of al-Jawa. His agent recognised me and was delighted I had come. We encountered favourable winds for ten days but when we were near the country of Tawalisi [Sulawesi?] the wind changed, the sky became dark, and there was heavy rain. For ten days we did not see the sun.

'Then we entered an unknown sea. The crew of the junk were frightened and wanted to return to China, but it was not possible. We spent forty-two days without knowing which sea we were in. At first light on the forty third day, a mountain became visible in the sea about twenty miles away. The wind was carrying us directly towards it. The sailors were amazed and said: "We are not near land, and there is no knowledge of a mountain in the sea. If the wind drives us on to it, we shall perish."

'Everyone resorted to self-abasement, to devotion, to renewed repentance, supplicating God in prayer. The merchants swore to give plentiful alms. The wind became somewhat calmed and then at sunrise we saw that the mountain had risen into the air and there was light between it and the sea. We were amazed at this and I saw the sailors weeping and saying goodbye to each other. I said "What is the matter?" They said: "What we took for a mountain is the Rukh. If it sees us we shall perish." We were less than ten miles off. Then God most High gave us the blessing of favourable wind which took us directly away from it.'

By now some of the elements are becoming familiar: first, a ship sails far out into the Great Encircling Ocean and makes it back again. Secondly, an unusual phenomenon of light or darkness is readily attributed by Islamic travellers in the Pacific to the Rukh. The critical piece of data in Ibn Battuta's account is the 'forty-two days'. If his junk sailed steadily west for 40 days, at say five knots with a following wind, it would have sailed thousands of kilometres and halfway across the Pacific.

There are a number of variables in this tale, and we have no idea of the average speed or the direction of his ship, but it is just possible that the mountain Ibn Battuta saw has already been mentioned in this book. The first tall peak visible to sailors approaching New Zealand from the tropics is Taranaki, halfway down the west coast of the North Island. It is an almost perfect cone, solitary, more than 2500 metres high, often white with snow, and it is standing on a cape: from three directions it appears to emerge from the sea. The perception that a mountain has risen into the air can be caused by refraction of light from the sea surface. If the mountain is also almost symmetrical, and white, then mariners who are already frightened and disposed to think about the demons and jinn known to live far out in the Great Encircling Ocean might well turn to the Rukh, or perhaps even its egg — and the Rukh's egg was said to be as large as a mountain — as the shape appears to rise slowly into the air.

It is about now, late in the thirteenth century, that the iconography of the Rukh approaches its final form. In the *Book of Marvels*, al-Qazwini tells another tale with strong echoes of the Second Voyage of Sindbad: 'A certain man of Isfahan got into debt, left his home and went to sea on a trading vessel which got caught in a great whirlpool in the Persian Sea. A wise man on board said that if one man gave up his life for the others they might be saved. The man from Isfahan asked a group of merchants on board whether they would pay his debts and look after his family if he gave up his life. To this they assented. The wise man explained they should sacrifice the man from Isfahan by abandoning him on a desert island nearby. Left on the island, the Isfahani saw a great bird perched in a tree. He watched it carefully for a few days and saw that every morning it flew away over the sea and returned at night. One morning, summoning his courage, he caught hold of the bird's talons and was carried aloft and over the water to the mainland where he dropped himself off and landed on the village haystack. The villagers were amazed at the visitation from the sky and the headman gave the man from Isfahan a great sum of money and so he returned home rich and happy ever after.'

In the oldest surviving copy of the *Marvels*, printed not long after 1300, the man is borne above ranges of watery hills by a kind of great white parrot with a tuft, related to the Anqa, and not unlike the ancient image of Garuda carved at Sanchi in central India.

A second manuscript of the *Marvels* was produced in Mosul about 1305. This time the illustration shows a large, combative, multi-coloured rooster, which was the standard Persian depiction of the Simurgh.

Twenty years later a third manuscript appeared, this one from Iran. Now the bird is dark-feathered and more markedly aquiline.

It would be easy to read too much into this. The dark-bodied eagle-type of 1320 may be a product of pure chance or artistic whim. Illustrators are a law unto themselves and follow their own instincts. In any case, Islam was a widely scattered mediaeval civilisation, and there was no longer a central clearing house for comparison of information. In 1258 the great city of Baghdad had fallen and the caliphate had ended; Iraq and Iran were both now parts of the Mongol empire and everything in the world was more fluid and uncertain than before.

Yet the unusual conformation of the body of the bird in the 1320 picture may point to an encounter with a real creature. In the Māori legend about the backward Nuku-mai-tore who were under attack from a great bird, the hero Pungarehu who came and saved them noted that as the predator came flying towards him that *its head was down.* It is an odd detail to have survived retelling in an oral tradition over many generations. The 2009 report on the CAT scan of the eagle's skull had this to say: 'The angle of the lateral semi-circular canals to the hard palate was higher in Haast's eagle than in related Accipitridae . . . suggesting a *downward tilt to the head.*'[30]

Could a physical detail of this kind, seen by an eyewitness, have come to the knowledge of an Arab or Persian artist in the early fourteenth century, and account for the curve in the bird's body as, almost tenderly, it carries its wide-eyed passenger through the gestural clouds?

Whatever the answer, it was there, among blue and white clouds in a scarlet sky, that the paper trail of words and images suggested by Professor Bivar comes to an end. There were no more signposts in his essay, and although stories about the Rukh continued to be told for centuries, there was no new data and no later encounters were reported, and although variations continued, the iconography of the Rukh, having arrived at the dark-feathered bird of prey, has generally remained there.

Towards the end of his essay, Professor Bivar admits the limitations of the written record. Language is a main source for knowledge of the past but it has drawbacks. Meanings shift and become obscure. Place-names are especially unstable: the locality of half the places mentioned by Ibn Battuta — and not just headlands, or distant mountains sighted from a deck, but cities and entire kingdoms (where was Tawalisi?) — is today uncertain.

Illustrations meanwhile are resolutely mute and open to different interpretation. Bivar makes it plain that in order to *prove* there was a sighting of the great eagle in the Southern Ocean, information of a different kind — heavy, solid, long-lasting — is needed. He cites the value of ancient anchors, for instance, found in Mediterranean harbours in helping us understand the maritime history and trade patterns of the Bronze Age. But no one has ever gone looking for mediaeval Asian anchors in the harbours of the South Pacific. Where would you start? If there was early travel from the northern hemisphere into the region it was extremely sporadic, and presumably unintended.

Yet at least one solid and apparently mediaeval object has been found in New Zealand, on the west coast of the North Island, and although its presence there has never been explained, seen in a certain light it appears to have a connection if not to the Rukh of the eagle type then to one of its close relations among the mythical birds of Asia.

Chapter 14

One morning in 1878, following a gale which had sprung up the day before and lasted all night, a man named Richard Nazer set out for a walk near Kāwhia, on the west coast of the North Island, to see what damage had been done. Nazer's father was an alderman in the channel port of Dover who became rich after he was granted by a special act of Parliament the right 'to light the streets of the town with flammable air'. An aura of gloom, by contrast, of comparative failure lingers over the son. Everything he did seemed to go wrong.

He immigrated to New Zealand in the 1850s and set up as a trader at lonely Aotea, a few kilometres north of Kāwhia. There are suggestions he was involved in gun-running to Māori and then had to abandon his property and flee when war between the races started. Auckland shipping reports tell us that in 1868 Nazer arrived at the port of Onehunga with 'two empty casks', and sailed out again with 'oats, flour and a bedstead'. For a while he was acting chairman of the Total Abstinence Society in Raglan but was then denounced as an impostor and had to resign: he wasn't a teetotaller at all, he just couldn't resist joining a club.

The family was often on the move. In Thames, things seemed to be looking up. Miss Nazer 'astonished the young men in town by her graceful skating', the local paper reported, and Nazer became a verger and taught Sunday school, but then his son George, fourteen, got into a fight with a butcher's boy named Henry and kicked him in the stomach. Henry died several days later. Peritonitis was the cause but public indignation ran high. The family was soon on the way out of town again. What Nazer was doing back on the west coast in 1878, inside the border of the King Country, a Māori enclave closed to Pākehā in the years of bitterness after the land wars, is unclear. Perhaps he returned to look at his old store, but by then store, house and garden were in a state of ruin.

Yet just for a moment, on the morning he stepped out to look around after a storm, Nazer's life lifted above the ordinary. He saw a tree which had blown over in the night and went to take a closer look. Among the roots there was a boulder of some kind. He bent down and picked it up and, brushing off the dirt, found himself looking at an extraordinary object — a carving of a bird in dark green stone, weighing a couple of kilograms, the wings closed, the body bent forward and the head low. The tree was later described as a 'very old manuka' although here the puzzles immediately set in, since mānuka doesn't grow very old, rarely living more than 50 years.

If the story so far sounds like a fairy tale — the night-long gale, the blown-down tree, a magical object among the roots

— maybe some of it is. A tangle of competing versions soon sprang up: it wasn't Nazer who found the bird, but a certain Māori who sold it to a man called Walker. Alternatively, it was found by a farmer named Naylor when he was digging fencepost holes. Or the Māori who found it *was* Albert Walker and the carving was a fake which he passed off as genuine to a Major Drummond-Hay and then skipped town for the South Sea Islands.

Among these brambles, one hard fact emerges. By 1881 the carving was in the possession of Drummond-Hay in the town of Cambridge on the banks of the Waikato River. Drummond-Hay was a licensed interpreter and occasional land dealer, and was described as a 'Pakeha-Maori', by which was meant a white who lived on very close terms with Māori. One day an elderly Māori woman of chiefly rank whose identity has not been handed down to us visited Drummond-Hay, saw the carving and then — it's a pity we don't know more, for it was an important moment — she *recognised* it. She didn't ask what it was, as she knew already. She asked only where it had been found.

'On hearing where it was discovered she bowed herself and sang a song relating to it.

> Kaore te aroha ki taku potiki
>
> Tuhana tonu ake, i te ahiahi
>
> Great is my love for this sweet thing
> That glows in the evening.'[31]

We know the song because over the next few months certain Māori grandees — King Tāwhiao, his first minister Te Ngakau and the great warrior chief Rewi Maniapoto — came to see the object and the same song was sung. The carving was identified by all these visitors as a treasure which had been missing for a long time, possibly for centuries.

Drummond-Hay then agreed to sell it to a former fellow officer, a Major Wilson, who presented it to his wife, Te Aorere, a young Māori woman of high rank who displayed it in her drawing room. Wilson had built a splendid house on the riverbank in Cambridge. Stables, gardens, a conservatory, innumerable flowers . . . Wilson was rich and in love. Te Aorere loved violets; violets therefore were everywhere.

Fifteen years earlier, Māori and Pākehā had been at war in this district. The settlers won the field and then stole — 'confiscated' — almost all the land in the region, and Major Wilson got his share. Yet Te Aorere presides in a drawing room where both races meet, the carving is on display, and the song is heard again and again. It turned out that it was known across the country, even in distant tribal areas, which was taken as evidence of its antiquity. In 1853, for instance, without knowing what its subject was, Governor Grey had published one version in his collection of Māori songs and legends.

Kaore te aroha ki taku potiki . . .

'Potiki', the beloved, the apple of the eye — that was how the carving was regarded. Rewi Maniapoto, we are told, 'took it away with him' — he appears to have been staying with the Wilsons and took it to his room, although the story is not clear and perhaps he left the house with it — and then woke several times in the night to 'tangi' over it. In the song, the bird is not named 'Korotangi' but 'Korotau', and 'Korota' in another version. There was no agreement on the meaning or origin of these names but all the visitors were of one mind about the thing itself: it was a great taonga, a treasure, it had been missing a long time, it had been in Māori possession for a long time before that, and also — perhaps most important — it was not Māori. The song emphasises this:

Ehara tena he manu maori

Me titiro ki te huruhuru whakairoiro mai no tawhiti

This is no Maori bird

Look at the feathers finely carved in a distant land.

Europeans took the same view. To most people who saw it, the closely incised feathers suggested Chinese or east Asian craftsmanship. Major Wilson sent the carving to Canterbury Museum where a cast was made and Julius von Haast wrote to the Royal Society: 'The bird has been carved with a sharp instrument, either of iron or of bronze, of which, as we know, the Maoris had no knowledge; the lines are all cut so evenly that it could not have been done with a stone implement.'

At the museum, Haast added, he had an ancient Japanese bronze bird 'the character of which is, in many respects, not unlike [this] specimen carved in stone. In both, the feathers on the back are rounded, with a central line, from which the smaller lines slope down on both sides, while the wing feathers are more pointed, and have a similar ornamentation. To my mind there is no doubt that they both have a somewhat similar origin, and come from the same eastern country or, if from two different countries, that the latter are nearly related to each other, and where, for many centuries, if not for thousands of years, industrial art has been practised.'[32]

If they were right, the Māori experts and Haast, then a mystery presented itself: how had the Korotangi reached New Zealand from east Asia hundreds of years ago? Tainui, the iwi or confederation of tribes living in and near the Waikato district, who claimed ownership of the stone bird, were adamant that it had been brought with their ancestors when they sailed from Hawaiki, but since bronze and iron tools were not known in eastern Polynesia and the statue resembled nothing made in that region, the mystery did not recede very far.

And there was the secondary question: what *was* the Korotangi? Haast first suggested it was a prion, which is a species of seabird, but he changed his mind on examining the nostril openings and decided it was a kind of duck. This was close to the Māori opinion. They saw a resemblance to the pūtangitangi, a small goose or shelduck which has a piercing and melancholy cry — or rather two cries, male and female having different calls which they make together as they fly, the male sounding like a trumpet (the pū) and the female the 'high note [tangitangi] of a clarionet'.[33]

Yet the sculptor had given the bird clawed feet, very

un-gooselike, and they are curled as if perching on the branch of a tree. Great disputes broke out at the Royal Society and beyond. Edward Tregear, a scholar of the Māori language, connected the bird to the dove of Noah: 'It is probably of immense antiquity (perhaps brought even from the very source of the Deluge-stories in far-off Asia); it may be quite the oldest relic of primitive men and their beliefs in existence.'

William Maskell, an entomologist with a special interest in scale beetles, on the other hand, said the Māori accounts were nothing but 'old women's fables', and assured the society that he himself attached no value whatsoever to any of their accounts: 'Beyond the date of a man's grandfather . . . the memory of savages does not, as a rule, go much further back. As to occurrences of earlier date, why, a Maori will manufacture legends by the score to order. Any number of European ships might have touched at New Zealand and from any of these the stone bird might have been stolen by the Maoris and made the subject of songs, of legends, and all sorts of rubbish.'

The suggestion was also made that the carving was a bird bath ornament which had lately arrived from Europe, probably Italy.

A prion, a duck, a goose, the dove of Noah, the most ancient artefact in existence, a bird bath ornament . . . no one really knew. Whatever it was, new legends began to gather around the object almost as soon as it was back in the daylight. Te Aorere Wilson was warned by Te Ngakau to throw it into the Waikato River and avoid the danger of an evil spell or bewitchment being cast on her by certain people who wanted to own the object themselves, Rewi Maniapoto — Te Aorere's uncle — being chief suspect in this regard. Te Aorere refused:

Korotangi must not be lost again. Two years later she was dead.

Naturally, people blamed the uncle, or the carving. Her funeral was the largest ever seen in the district. 'For three days almost all the shops here were partially closed and flags were hoisted at half-mast over the town on the day of her death,' the press reported. 'At least sixty carriages, over a hundred horseman and altogether a thousand people on foot followed the funeral . . . Many well-known colonists were present and there were naturally large numbers of Māori women dressed in mourning and wearing green leaves, and forming a very picturesque part of the procession.'

The Korotangi was bequeathed to Te Aorere's son and occasionally put on display in Cambridge, but was then deposited in a bank vault in Wellington for safe keeping and finally lent to the Dominion Museum on the stipulation that it was never locked away in the dark. During the Second World War this edict was forgotten and the carving was packed up and sent to the basement against the threat of Japanese air raids. The Japanese did not bomb Wellington but, according to one apocryphal tale, messages soon arrived from the Waikato asking why the Korotangi could not see daylight. The descendants of the Wilsons, 500 kilometres away, had sensed its demotion. It was brought back upstairs and put in a glass case on the first landing of the museum's main staircase, where it remained for the next 50 years, and which is where I saw it for the first time one rainy afternoon when I was a student in Wellington.

Chapter 15

I should have been in the law library, I suppose, that afternoon, but for me the attraction of the law library was not high. I never felt at home there and worse than that I felt that everyone else, including even the stained-glass figure of Richard the Lion Heart who for some reason presided in the gothic window high above the law students' heads, knew I didn't really belong. I was a sort of impostor, only pretending to be interested in torts and crimes and contract law. *Thump* went the great leather-bound volumes of reports down on oak desks, *thump, thump* — my classmates were eagerly tracking down case law but I never experienced the exhilaration of this.

Instead, after an hour or two, I would slip away, out the door, down the steps and off into the afternoon. Where to? It didn't really matter. I might go to Parliament and listen from the gallery, or catch the train to Paekākāriki and walk along the beach, or mooch around the second-hand bookshops in

Courtenay Place and Cuba Street where, by four in the afternoon, the hookers were starting to squall with the sailors. One afternoon I walked across town in the rain to the old Dominion Museum on Buckle Street and on the first landing of the stairs saw a single object in its own glass case: a bird of dark green stone, head bent low as if bowed over its secrets. This was the Korotangi.

It was a winter's day — a cold blank light filled the staircase window. The staircase, I suppose, was a sign of embarrassment. A museum is fundamentally classificatory, and the Korotangi, alone in its waist-high glass case on the landing, was a problem. It clearly did not belong in the elaborate gloom — as it seemed that afternoon — of the Māori collection with its great canoes and carved whare behind me. But no one knew where it did belong, and that was what I liked most about it. *Over how many miles of ocean have the carved wings flown?* Here was something worth thinking about, far more interesting to me than the problems of torts and contracts, which in any case had already been answered by long-dead law lords, if only you could track them down.

I did not, as far as I remember, stumble on the Korotangi by chance: I already knew it was in Buckle Street and went over in the rain that day to look for it. Forty years later, when I was thinking about Professor Bivar and the value he placed on archaeology in establishing historical facts, I thought of the Korotangi and opened an old notebook I had kept as a sort of diary when I was student and, to my surprise — for this is rare in any research — immediately found what I was looking for.

```
        Great is my love for this sweet thing
that glows in the evening.
   But it has gone,Iam alone
    In this empty house.Look,my dear,one
    At the birds floating thre e.They are nothing
    They are common birds,.The carved wings ,
    The stone feathers of the Korot u have flown
    Over many more miles of ocean -
    None  now where he has been
    Nor where he is gone.Was he seen
```

I was a terrible typist — I can count eight errors, mostly involving the space-bar, in the first four lines. I didn't own a typewriter and must have borrowed one to type out this translation of the song to the Korotangi which I had found in an anthology of Māori verse, although which machine it was and who it belonged to — I remember a portable Olympus in a smart green case, and an old ex-office machine with a deep black well out of which the keys sprang up to hit the paper with heavy pecks like the first drops of rain before a downpour — those details have now gone, but standing on the staircase in the museum looking down at the carved feathers in the cold winter light, I already knew the questions the Korotangi raised . . . *None know where he has been nor where he is gone.*

The song had been composed during the period when the carving was missing, and was therefore out of date. We now knew where he had been. He had been under the roots of a mānuka tree somewhere near Kāwhia. But where had he come from in the first place? How and why had he been brought to Aotearoa? Those questions were still resistant to enquiry when I went to the museum to look at the carving. What year this was, my first or second or third at law school, I cannot now remember, and the old notebook gave me no clue. It was a disreputable object in any case — both cardboard covers detached, the whole thing tied together with piece of white silk torn from an RAF airman's scarf I once bought in a second-hand shop, so it was more like a compendium than a notebook — loose papers, photographs, press clippings, a sketch in blue ink of a cross-section of the human eye, and the complete lyrics, for some reason, of 'Under the Boardwalk' by the Drifters, all jammed in together with no thought of order or chronology.

Yet when I opened it, and the Korotangi poem came to hand, two other pages fluttered out, two portraits done in pen and ink, and I immediately felt they also had a part to play in the story. Appearing from the same level of the midden, so to speak, I first thought they might help put a date on the typescript and the visit to the museum, and I remembered exactly who had done them and where and when.

It was in the last week of my third and last year in Wellington. I was feeling happy that day because my best friend, whose name was Jim Vivieaere, had just arrived from Dunedin on his way north for the summer. That night he and I and Jane, the girl he was travelling with, stayed up very late talking, mostly about our futures — he was at medical school and as unhappy there as I was at law school — while the wind, the endless Wellington wind, prowled around the house testing the window panes, and as we talked Jim dashed off these lightning sketches, one of me with pen in hand and a notebook on my knee, and one of Jane who was in a truculent mood that night and was wearing a school gym-slip as a sign of general rebelliousness, and in the morning I found the sketches on the kitchen table and put them away in the notebook and then forgot all about them until they reappeared with the Korotangi poem.

Of course as a dating reference, it didn't take long for me to realise they were of no use at all. The notebook was far less well organised than a midden, where everything lies more or less in chronological order. Yet all the same, when I looked at them and remembered the night we stayed up talking, with the wind rushing outside the house, I had a strong intuition that there *was* a connection between Jim, who was Cook Islands Māori, and the Korotangi, or rather that, through Jim, some new information about it would come to hand. And furthermore, he had a part to play, an important and conclusionary part, in the whole book I was writing, this book, on the eagle.

What these contributions might be I couldn't imagine, and I couldn't call him to discuss the subject, as Jim had died not long before, rather unexpectedly, and comparatively young. And since I had no idea how he could help me, I could do nothing but wait and see what turned up.

I did not have to wait long. I was still pursuing the Korotangi theme, and spent several weeks looking at bird imagery of eastern Polynesia, from where the carving had been brought by the ancestors of Tainui, but I could find nothing remotely like it in any of the Tahitian sources I looked at and I was about to give up that line of enquiry when I read that, for the Tainui people, Hawaiki, their original homeland, meant a particular island named Raiatea, 100 kilometres west of

Tahiti. And I then remembered standing on a low headland on Raiatea one day with Jim Vivieaere — this was about 25 years after the night he and I sat up so late talking — and Jim made a strange assertion which I thought at the time was not only extremely unlikely but, in the circumstances, highly comical, which was in fact the only reason the incident had stayed in my mind.

The reason we were both on Raiatea that day was as follows. I had just resigned from a newspaper in London and as a kind of leaving gift the travel editor offered me a commission to go to different islands in Polynesia and write a short series of pieces for her pages. We settled on Tahiti, Tonga and Sāmoa, and then a few days before I was to fly out from Auckland to Tahiti I realised that the airline which provided free tickets, and the tourist boards which arranged the accommodation, would have no objection if I took a photographer along.

I didn't really need a photographer — in fact I knew quite well that the picture desk on the newspaper jealously guarded its right to provide images for every story and rejected, on the flimsiest pretext, any pictures that a writer might come up with. On the other hand, I had been to the South Pacific islands before and knew that travelling there was very different if you were in the company of a Polynesian. Doors open. And so I asked Jim if he would like to come on a short trip to Tahiti as a 'press photographer'. He agreed, and we arrived in Papeete and sailed to Raiatea two days later.

I had chosen Raiatea because it was off the beaten track, comparatively speaking — I had no interest in describing the luxury resorts with their glass-floored fale standing on stilts in the lagoons of Bora Bora or Moorea. I also had a vague idea that Raiatea had once been the holy island, 'sacred Raiatea': I knew for instance that one of the finest churches built by Māori after missionaries arrived in New Zealand was named 'Rangiātea' after the island, and that the altar of this church, in Ōtaki, was sited directly above a basket of earth or stones brought from Raiatea centuries before. Why did Raiatea have this special status? I wanted to go there to see if there was anything that could still be detected in the landscape or the atmosphere, as people say they feel at Iona or Glastonbury or the isle of Patmos, or in the gorges of Delphi where lightning sometimes flashes out of a blue sky in the middle of the day . . .

Jim and I arrived in Raiatea accordingly and set off, writer and photographer, to explore the island. And then . . . nothing. The French had been in residence in Raiatea for a century or more and a deep suburban torpor reigned. We drove around the whole island clockwise in about 50 minutes and then, to unwind, drove around anti-clockwise. A horse drowsed over a gate near a house with closed green shutters. A wavelet broke on the sand. The palms shuffled in the breeze and then fell still. Hymns sounded from a church with unglazed windows.

I was operating on the principle (highly debatable) that the less I knew about the place the better: I wanted to keep the screen blank, so to speak, unclouded by preconceptions, in the hope that I would detect any track of the sacred, the *tapu*, and so I read nothing, not even the brochures in the hotel lobby. This system, however, did not seem to be working. Raiatea not only did not give up its secrets — it seemed to have none.

Nor did any doors open. Jim had acquired a new and rather

forbidding manner since I had last seen him. He had given up med school and gone on to art school, had a creditable career as an artist and then became a curator and set up the first group show of Polynesian artists, mostly young and urban. *Bottled Ocean* was a huge success. It travelled the country and made Jim's name. Like Prospero, he had discovered a whole world of new spirits. The great exhibition *Oceania* which opened at the Royal Academy in London in 2018 was in part his brainchild although he did not live to see it.

I saw a change in him when we met at Auckland Airport about to fly out to Papeete.

Jim was travelling very light.

'Where's your camera?'

'What camera?'

'You're the photographer, remember?'

'I despise photography.'

'*Do* you? I didn't know that. Could you, um, pretend not to despise it, just for a few minutes? Just while we meet the Air New Zealand guys. Here — take mine.'

'That?' said Jim, marvelling at my cheap Minolta. 'Well, if I was going to take photographs, I wouldn't use *that*.'

I needn't have worried. The airline people who came to meet us and hand over our business-class tickets were too awed by Jim's grand manner to question his credentials. The same could be said of the immigration officers he met at Papeete airport. This was *his* world. What were they doing, his scornful expression said, two rotund Frenchmen guarding the gates of the citadel of eastern Polynesia?

Once we reached Raiatea Jim walked around the streets of the little capital, Uturoa, like a king inspecting a backward and frankly unsatisfactory part of his realm. It was to me that the locals came up and asked quietly, 'Qui est monsieur?'

Monsieur and I were largely left to our own devices.

I wasn't particularly worried. Travel writing is the least demanding of genres. You can write anything. You can write that there was nothing to write about. I could describe the croissants, of Parisian quality, on sale at the Uturoa bakery, or the Raiatean girls dancing on the backs of beflowered lorries on Bastille Day, or the strange sensation, crossing a glass-floored fale in the middle of the night and seeing coloured fish dart below your feet as in a diagram of the unconscious. In the meantime, Jim and I had found something more important to discuss. We caught up.

We had been close as teenagers, members of a little group, a gang of four, who met when we were about fifteen and living in Napier. Later, when girlfriends arrived and cousins came to stay for the summer, the gang might expand to ten or twelve but then it contracted again and we four — Jim, Barry ('Spaz'), Malcolm and I — stayed close at university and for years afterwards. But eventually our careers took us on different paths and to different parts of the world and in the end even major events in each of our lives became vague and distant to the others, bulletins from far away.

The major event in Jim's life during the last ten years was this: he had met his parents.

Of the four of us in the gang, three lived in ordinary nuclear families in ordinary wooden villas up and down the hilly Napier streets, but Jim was different. He lived in the mansion at the top of the hill with a red Daimler parked under the portico and an indoor cinema with a curtain of green and gold brocade which opened and closed at the touch of a button. Jim, however, was a sort of foundling. He had been given up for adoption at birth, and for the first twelve years of his life went bobbing through a series of foster homes until he found safe haven in the mansion at the top of the hill. He did not know who or where his real parents were. This gave him, in our eyes, the prestige of mystery. And also of liberty. I remember feeling envious when I heard that Jim, at about the age of ten, had changed his own surname, adding a second 'v' and extra 'e's, and that no one — neither the state, his official guardian, nor his foster parents at the time — even noticed. This seemed to me an exemplary state of freedom. *Nobody noticed.*

Jim was also more mature than us. We all leave home in the end, and teenagers engage in that prospect with awe and fascination. Jim was miles ahead. He had left 'home' in effect at birth, and had never looked back. He refused, under some pressure, ever to call his wealthy foster parents Mum and Dad. They were good, well-meaning people and he was grateful to them and he kept up the connection all his life, but they always looked slightly baffled by this talented personage who arrived in their midst. His foster brothers all left school as soon as they could and went into the family business, which was car repair. There were no books in the mansion, but the family did not know that because they called magazines 'books' and a few *Popular Mechanics* were generally lying around. The only film that was ever played, to my knowledge, in the cinema with the concertina curtain was *The Ten Commandments* with Charlton Heston in the lead as Moses.

Jim, by contrast, was always near the top of his class, good at sports, artistic, creative, vastly entertained by and curious about the world. In the sixth form he took a lead role in the school play, which that year was *The Merchant of Venice*. His Shylock caused a sensation. He played the old money-lender with energy, and venom, and sympathy. Perhaps as an outsider himself, the only Polynesian in our middle-class white world, and one who was also excluded from local Māori life, he identified with the Jew at bay among the Christians.

Hearing distant acclaim, his foster parents felt they should go and see the play. They had never been to the theatre before and certainly not to Shakespeare. On the way home that night his foster mother turned around to face Jim in the back of the Daimler, his hair still white with makeup powder.

'We didn't understand one word,' she said bitterly. 'Not a *single* word!'

The next day he told us this story.

'Not — a — *single* — word,' he said delightedly, his face crinkled up with laughter. His hair was still white. The powder was supposed to indicate Shylock's old age but gave Jim, at seventeen, a princely and exotic appearance of which he was fully aware. He didn't brush it out for days.

As to his real parents, they were a subject mentioned only occasionally.

'I'm probably royal or something,' he said carelessly, if the matter came up. This turned out to be not far from the truth.

Driving around the coastal road of Raiatea, he told me the full story. He had found his mother first. It turned out that for all those years he was growing up in Hawke's Bay she was not far away. Her story was a sad one. A very pretty girl, she grew up on one of the outer islands of the Cook Islands group, and in her teens went to live in the little capital Avarua on the main island of Rarotonga. There she became pregnant. The father of the child was a young man of high rank, related to the royal line. This alone was cause for scandal. Polynesian societies are highly stratified, some almost vertical in fact, like the mountain of Bora Bora which, driving the coastal road of Raiatea, we could sometimes see far away over the sea like a pillar holding up the sky.

To make matters worse, Jim's father was already engaged to someone of suitable rank. But now his first born would be a child of *low degree*, conceived not on the chiefly mat but probably outside somewhere, under the moon and glimmering palms. Nothing more shocking could be imagined. There was only one solution: the young mother-to-be was hustled out of sight. She was put on the boat to New Zealand, sent to a rural hospital to give birth and immediately, presumably under orders, gave up her son for adoption, and Jim began his long journey through the homes of people of another race while his mother was left to shift for herself.

The modern tide of migration from Pacific islands to New Zealand had not started by then and there was no Rarotongan community she could turn to. Instead, she ended up in a Māori world, in this case in Palmerston North, two hours' drive from Napier, and she had been there ever since.

Things had not gone well for her. Jim mentioned a broken marriage, perhaps instanced with domestic violence. I had a picture of broken windows, raised voices, dead cars on the lawn. Perhaps it was not as bad as that, but it was a world, in any case, completely foreign to Jim's experience, riding to church in the Daimler, med school, art school, exhibitions in Germany and Taiwan, artist-in-residence in the Moët &

Chandon chateau in the misty fields of Champagne . . .

His mother was happy to find him again — her lost first born! — but I got the impression that she was too tired by life to rise to the occasion. We stopped at the side of the road and Jim showed me a recent photo. An elderly woman with a sweet and timid expression but, above all, weary . . .

'She can't get it together,' said Jim.

'How old is she?'

'Sixty-four.'

'Can't you help?'

'What can *I* do? None of them can get it together. They're all still in Palmerston North. I had an exhibition there and asked two of my half-brothers along. The opening ceremony was quite emotional and one started to blub and the other went all grim and stern. He's the one who does ju-jitsu—'

'What does the first one do?'

'The blubbery one?'

'Yes, what does he do?'

'He goes down to the river for driftwood. He's on the dole. He's got five kids to look after. His wife hung herself. She was from the East Coast. She got depressed.'

It was strange to hear Jim talking about his brothers and sisters. When we were young he was the essential isolate, and now he had four families — his own wife and daughters, his foster parents and their sons, his newly found real mother and half-siblings in Palmerston North. And then there was the fourth. They were the ones who now occupied his thoughts. From his mother he had learned the identity of his father. He flew to Rarotonga, went to the address he had been given and walked in.

His father looked at him in surprise, since he knew everyone on the island, but he said pleasantly: 'And who are you?'

'I'm Jim.'

'Who?'

It had not crossed Jim's mind that his father may never have known his name.

'I'm your son. Your eldest.'

'*What*? What do you want? You better go away. My wife doesn't even know you exist.'

It was a terrible moment. I realised Jim had been thinking about this meeting all his life. He admitted that he then became obsessed with his father. He stalked the old man when the latter came to Auckland, to a funeral, for example. Jim stood at the back of the crowd outside the church and held up a camera, snapping away like a press photographer into the window of a prison van.

We stopped on the side of the road again and he showed me the result: a small, dark man coming down the church steps with a grim countenance. This little nobleman on his plinth of earth in mid-ocean — Rarotonga is only a few miles across — had given Jim his life but also darkened it from the beginning and had no plans to make amends. Jim flew back to Rarotonga several times and tracked down other members of the family. Some of his half-siblings refused to have anything to do with him but others relented.

'At least they talk to me,' Jim said. 'They say, "Why are you chasing your father?" and I say, "I might want some land. I'm his first born. Or maybe I don't want any land. Maybe I just want acknowledgement. Maybe I don't even want that. When he dies, I'll just turn up at the funeral and carry the coffin.

They can't stop me doing that." That's what I told Manny.'

'Who's Manny?'

'My uncle. He's the one with power. He's the minister of something or other, I don't know — foreign minister or minister of health. He's on a bad trip though. He has this beautiful young wife and every day she cooks Manny dinner and goes off and stays the night with her lover and comes back in the morning. She gets away with it because he's a minister of something and doesn't want publicity. He's on the right-hand side of the family tree — they go straight back to the royal line.'

This was our main subject of conversation as we drove around Raiatea, about 800 kilometres east of Rarotonga, Jim talking on in a low monotone about his new sisters and brothers and uncles and aunts and his real parents and step-parents, and as he talked he opened his eyes very wide from time to time like someone who is trying to stay awake and keep seeing what is in front of him.

Meanwhile our time on Raiatea was running out and I still had not found my subject. On our last morning we drove out once more, and this time I turned down a side road where a signpost pointed to a place named Taputapuatea: I had seen the name on postcards on sale in Uturoa and had avoided it on that basis alone. I dreaded the sight of a line of tourist coaches. But again, I needn't have worried. There were no coaches and no one in view at all when we parked at the end of the lane and walked out under the trees onto a wide stony courtyard by the sea.

The stones were sun-blackened and rounded slightly like

turtle shells, and there was a sea wall of jagged stones like broken teeth. It was late morning, almost noon, very hot and very still. In Greece they talk of the noon-tide demon that lives among the rocks and can be glimpsed out of the corner of your eye, but here, in far Polynesia, who or what was present? Jim walked out over the stony marae and I went the other way and looked over the sea wall.

Nothing was moving: there was a great hush in the air and the sea was as still and silent as a sea in a painting. But something was out hunting, because just then a school of little fish jumped out of the water in a single arc, as if to see who was passing by, then fell back with a sound like silk ripping.

Then Jim called out.

'Over here.'

'What?'

'Come over.'

He was standing by a tall white pillar of stone in the middle of the marae.

'Take a photo of me,' he said.

'What?'

'Take a photo of me,' he said, 'by this stone.'

I felt some hilarity at this. Here was the photographer who 'despised photography' and refused to take any pictures himself, but who now required a photograph after all — one of him, to be taken by the writer. I started to laugh but Jim's expression made me think again.

'Take a picture of me here,' he said again. *I know my ancestors were here.*

He looked so serious that I forgot to ask how he could possibly know such a thing, or to point out that we had just spent four days talking about his ancestors who had lived on another island hundreds of miles away. Instead, I duly complied, took a picture of Jim by the white pillar and put the camera away.

Then I largely forgot about the incident until the time came, about fifteen years later, when it struck me that Jim had something to tell me about the Korotangi, and I remembered that moment at Taputapuatea. The incident was still listed under 'comedy' in my mind, and that, I thought, was the only reason I remembered it, as if memory, which is frequently accused of playing tricks and losing files, is more like a clever director who sets up a scene, as farce for instance (Jim did not, in fact, 'despise photography' and often used a camera in his own art), so that one day, perhaps far in the future, it will come to mind when needed.

This time I didn't laugh, or ignore the possible implications of his claim, and decided to look more closely at the history of Raiatea, and in particular of Taputapuatea. It did not take long to learn that the stony courtyard was once a place of immense importance across much of the Pacific, and that in itself had a bearing not perhaps on the provenance of the Korotangi, but on its progress across the ocean from its original and unknown source.

Chapter 16

'On the eve of the great day, the clergy of the royal marae held sacred vigils throughout the night at Taputapuatea. This was called *pure toiaha, pure iri ani a te tahu'a* — "weighty prayers, prayers with chilly skin of the priests" — and as the morning was ushered in the gods were said to be flying and whistling around the marae and all over the district. Soon upon the sea and along the shore a semi-barbarous pageantry took place. A long flotilla bearing nude men and women of the *arioi* headed by the new *anuanua* (rainbow) or sacred canoe of the god [came into shore] ... The canoe had a platform towards the centre for the god 'Oro and the coming sovereign. The heralds, called *running meteors* and the people on shore were arrayed in their best attire, decked in wreaths and garlands. Then came the solemn procession from Taputapuatea inland to the great sacred white stone pillar, *te-papa-o-ruea* (the rock of investment).'

This description of a ceremony at Taputapuatea hundreds of years ago was written by Teuira Henry, a Tahitian ethnologist whose book, *Ancient Tahiti*, was based on the information her English grandfather collected in the 1820s and 1830s from priests and chieftains in Tahiti, Bora Bora and Raiatea when the ancient religion was still alive.

The name Taputapuatea is significant. 'Tapu', obviously, means 'sacred' but 'tapu-tapu' does not just mean doubly sacred. It had a particular connotation. It was reserved for places where human lives were taken as sacrifice. Despite the picture painted by eighteenth-century Europeans of a terrestrial paradise, war and human sacrifice were endemic in the Society Islands. A royal investiture at Taputapuatea, for example, required three living victims in rapid succession when new feathers were sown into the maro, a sacred girdle with a backing of perforated cloth, worn by the new sovereign.

'In each little hole,' Henry writes, 'the stem of a red feather was set, caught in lock stitch on the opposite side with a long, polished needle of human bone and set closely to the next one to imitate bird's plumage. The sacred needle was never taken from the work which was intended to last forever. A human victim was sacrificed for the perforating of the cloth, for the first putting in of the needle, and for the completing of the *maro*. It is said the gods manifested their approval by sending flashes of lightning upon the scene. The *to'ere*, a high drum about a foot in diameter, was beaten with different strokes to mark the beginning and the close of the offering of the human victim.'

Other occasions requiring a human death at Taputapuatea included the washing of the royal first born; an accidental tearing of the royal flag; introduction of the royal child to the public; circumcision of the first born prince or princess; provision of canoe-rollers — human bodies — at the commencement of a royal tour; awakening 'Oro, god of war, to preside over a battle; cheering up a king after a military defeat; and building a house of sacred treasures on the marae, in which case a human body, possibly of a child, was placed in each of the four holes dug for the corner posts.

These practices were not universal in Polynesia and were certainly not immemorial. A time was remembered, Henry tells us, when human sacrifice was unknown. 'Before the Flood, the world was luxuriant and the people were in the favour of the gods . . . But there came a time when there was a great drought and excessive heat in Raiatea, so that the people exclaimed, "Ta'aroa [the god Tangaroa] the Unique-Foundation, is angry; he is consuming us!" The king, moved to pity for his people, told the priests to pray and present offerings to Ta'aroa and obtain rain from heaven to restore the land.'

This was done with 'offerings of lean pigs, fish and bird's feathers', no fruit or other crops being available. But the drought continued: 'Then the king said, "We must humble ourselves before the god, we must tremble with fear! Let us offer a man as a tapu [pledge or sacrifice] to atone for unintentional offences." So the priests slew a man and offered him at the shrine of Ta'aroa and soon clouds gathered in the sky and rain fell and restored the land to its former flourishing condition. Thus it was shown that the gods liked human flesh and it remained the custom for the king or high priest to decide when such a sacrifice was required. But this happened very seldom until 'Oro, god of war, came into favour after the Flood.'

The evolution of religion is often obscure but in this instance, on Raiatea, it can be seen with some clarity. Taputapuatea was sacred because, like Delos, it was the birthplace of the greatest gods. There were millions of deities in Polynesia. Monotheism is said to have arisen in the bareness of the desert where nothing moves by day except the sun, and at night the flock of stars. On a richly forested tropical island, where the noise from the reef day and night sounds like traffic in a big city, a multiplication of spirits was inevitable. In the Hawaiian version of the story of the voyaging Rata, for instance, when the first tree has been cut down and must then be put back in place, the little people of the forest, the Me-ne-hu-ne, come chanting:

> O the 4,000 gods!
> O the 40,000 gods!
> O the 400,0000 gods!
> O gods of these woods,
> Of the mountain, the knoll, the pine cone
> Of the dam of the watercourse,
> O, descend!

And all this for just one tree restoration . . . Among the 400,000 deities, a small number were pre-eminent. Ta'aroa or Tangaroa was the creator of the universe, and lord of the deeps, meaning both ocean and Milky Way. His son Tane was god of mankind, beauty and the forest. Tu, god of war, and Rongo, of peace, were also very powerful. Below these four came swarms of lesser divinities — there was a god of hairdressing, a god who painted the patterns on fishes, a god called Towering Wave who caused a single high breaker far out at sea; there was a god of quagmires — 'he was mottled, resembled a man, dwelled in mud, and on dark nights shot up into the air with great force' — and a god known only as Racket, who lived in the mountains and 'made a loud sound like the report of a cannon fired on a clear, windy day'. Racket (probably the detonation of volcanic rock heated by the sun) was last heard in Tahiti one afternoon in 1891, alarming both Tahitians and French settlers.

There was Oro-pa-aa, a particular spirit pervading the blue depths of the ocean: 'He has a roaring voice but no one has ever understood what he says. He lies with his head upward; the white foaming breakers are his jaws; he swallows anyone despite their station in life. He does not spare princes. He has never been known to say "that is enough".'

Here religion almost has the role of lyric poetry. Any sharp new perception of nature is codified, so to speak, and placed in a pantheon in order to be remembered.

The emergence of a new god is generally wrapped in mystery. All-powerful Ta'aroa was said to have been born near Taputapuatea or at least first appeared on Earth there, or nearby at Opoa, 'inserting his phallus' into the earth, at which point 'thunder sounded at Opoa'. What exactly happened to make this story is quite unclear. It has the dreamlike quality of all creation myths. But much later a second great god appeared at the same place, or rather a lesser god, named 'Oro, abruptly increased in power and this time the glint of hard fact can be seen.

One account of 'Oro's rise states that first there came a great flood. Since this happened at Taputapuatea, which is on a low headland, a tsunami may be meant. Tsunamis were — and are — the dread of the Polynesians. A Māori account from about the same period in the Cook Strait region: 'One night the monsters of the deep appeared and then the sea arose and Oh! my friends, it overwhelmed these people. Thousands of men, women and children were overwhelmed and buried in the sea by these monsters.'

In Raiatea, the flood was evidently followed by social unrest and then a religious revolution. The old gods were in retreat. Ta'aroa did not quite vanish but his favourite son, Tane, was displaced by 'Oro. Earlier 'Oro was a minor god of dance and the erect penis ('Oro means desire) and patron of warriors and comedians — a little god of testosterone, in other words, who, if we had tutelary gods today, might be blamed for brawls outside nightclubs.

In Raiatea, however, he became all-powerful. Different scenarios may be imagined. After a natural disaster, the youngest and strongest seize the resources, kill anyone who stands in their way and then see no need to give up this pleasing policy. Violence becomes institutionalised. The cult of 'Oro was extremely violent, and proselytising. The priests of the old gods Ta'aroa and Tane were driven away or killed by the followers of the new god. The whole of Raiatea was conquered and then, after widespread fighting, 'Oro took the main island of Tahiti itself, and the nearby islands of Bora Bora and Moorea.

The cult then spread to the Tuamotu Archipelago in the east, the Austral Islands to the south, to Mangaia and

Rarotonga in the west, perhaps to the island of Rotuma further west and north of Fiji, to New Zealand — 'Aotearoa of the Maori' as the Tahitians called it — and there is evidence that devotees of 'Oro also came from the Marquesas and Hawai'i to take part in the ceremonies at Taputapuatea.

Teuira Henry describes one such gathering. First, canoes from around the Pacific assembled in the night on the eastern horizon and at daybreak advanced in double file, sounding conch shell trumpets and the deep-toned drum called Tangimoana (Sounding Sea). On shore the old, the infirm, women, children and domestic animals had already retired into the forest, out of harm's way.

'It was an occasion of awful solemnity . . . All was still along the shore, even the sea and elements which, tradition states, were hushed in unison for the festivity of the god . . . Across the bows connecting each double canoe was a floor covering chambers containing idols, drums, trumpets and other treasures for the gods and people of Raiatea, and on the floor were rows of sacrifices from abroad, human victims brought for the purpose and newly slain, and great fishes newly caught. They were placed on the floor alternately, a man and a cavalli fish, a man and a shark, a man and a turtle and finally a man.'[34]

These canoes came silently to shore and were met by the king and the two high priests or primates who represented the territories known as the Dark Lands and the Light Lands to the east and west where 'Oro was worshipped: 'On the road to the inner marae were laid as rollers the bodies of the slain men and over them were drawn the canoes still carrying idols and treasures . . . All set to work silently disposing of the sacrifices, strung through the hands with sennit and suspended on the boughs of the trees, the fish diversifying the spectacle of human bodies, and the priests of 'Oro chanted:

> Now eat of your long-legged fish
> 'Oro, O my king,
> Fighting warrior'

Henry provides a startling account of an incident at Taputapuatea which brought an end to the Alliance of Dark Lands and Light Lands: 'After the ritual and when the feasting had begun, a quarrel arose between the Primate of the Light Lands, Pa'oa'atea, and a high chief of the Dark Lands, who grew fierce and slew [the Primate]. Then another chief of the Light Lands named Te-Mauri-Arioi asked what had happened to the high priest.

'"I killed him."

'The second chief was enraged, rushed forward and struck the Primate of the Dark Lands, who fell down as if dead. Great anger and confusion between the two sides followed and there might have been more bloodshed had not the people of Te-ao-tea [the Light Lands] at once taken to their canoes and fled. They rushed precipitately forward into the bay . . . and not looking to the right towards the sacred harbour by which they had recently entered with much pagan pomp they fled . . . Thus ended the friendly alliance which long had united many kindred islands.'[35]

In the 1830s an English missionary named John Williams heard the same story in Raiatea but with added details. The people of an island named Rarotonga, he was told, 'made a large drum, called Ta'i-moana, or Sounds of the Seas, which they sent by the hands of two priests, as a present to 'Oro . . . And after the priests had dedicated Tai-moana, some untoward circumstances occurred which induced the Raiateans to kill them. The gods were so enraged that persons who brought so valuable a present [were killed] that they took up the island [of Rarotonga] and "carried it completely away".'[36]

Williams was intrigued by this tale and set out to visit the unknown land. No one could find it for a long time, but eventually he arrived on Rarotonga. When the people there heard that there was a Raiatean on board Williams' ship he was besieged by questioners. 'One enquired where Tai-moana, the great drum, was, which the two priests Paoaui and Pao-atea took to Raiatea. Another demanded "Why did you Raiateans kill those men whose death induced the gods to remove our island to its present position?"'

Why indeed? None of the accounts state the reason for the quarrel. The Māori scholar Te Rangi Hīroa suggests it was a theological difference and implies it had to do with the number of sacrificial deaths demanded by the priests of 'Oro. He visited Taputapuatea in 1929 and was oppressed by gloom. To him the place seemed intensely sad. 'I tried to imagine the fight described by Te Uira Henry and the scattering of the Alliance . . . I saw Turi [captain of the *Aotea* canoe which returned to New Zealand] and others leaving the land reeking with the blood of human victims . . . saying to themselves "To hell with their stone marae with their human victims."'[37]

Afterwards in both Rarotonga and New Zealand human sacrifice continued, but it was never on the industrial scale required by 'Oro, and no vast stone marae were built.

Tangaroa, Lord of the Deeps, and Tane, his son, were restored to pre-eminence in both places. 'Oro, if he continued as a god at all, was under very changed circumstances: a little god named Koro is sometimes mentioned but he was now a female and in charge of dancing.

Rarotonga meanwhile had been 'carried completely away'. Of course it stayed where it always was; its 'removal' was just a way of saying that travel to Raiatea had become impossible. People usually make up after a quarrel, but a doctrinal difference is another matter, and it seems from John Williams' story about the Raiateans arriving in Rarotonga that, perhaps for centuries, there was hardly any contact between the two islands that had once seemed so close.

While I was reading this material, I began to think about the photograph I had taken of Jim, another Rarotongan visiting Taputapuatea. I couldn't remember how it had turned out and I wanted to see it again but I couldn't find it with the other pictures I had taken in Raiatea. Since Jim by this time was no longer alive, I wrote to his daughter, Cypress, asking her to send me a copy, but Cypress couldn't find it either. It then dawned on me that perhaps I couldn't remember what it looked like because I had never seen it. And sure enough, in a side pocket of the envelope containing my Raiatean pictures there were a few negatives I had never had developed.

So it was about fifteen years after Jim and I walked out into the noontide hush at Taputapuatea that I saw him there again, standing by the white stone of investiture where he was sure his ancestors had been before him. How he came by this insight I never knew but looking at it — it was a very bad photograph, blurred and out of focus — I thought my intuition had been right and that Jim had indeed provided a new detail in the story of the Korotangi, for it was clear that he was also right: during the era of the Alliance of Dark Lands and Light Lands, his ancestors, at least those in the royal line of Rarotonga, would undoubtedly have made their way to Taputapuatea and stood by the same white pillar. And that fact had some bearing on the travels of the Korotangi.

For generations (no one is sure when the alliance began or ended), Taputapuatea was the equivalent of Delphi in the eastern Mediterranean — an international shrine where people came from all points of the horizon carrying gifts for the god. And if a ship from east Asia, for example, sailed below the equator and happened to be carrying a bird carved in dark green stone, it need only touch at one of the many islands where 'Oro was worshipped, strung like a net across millions of square kilometres of ocean, for the carving plausibly to end up in the central treasury of 'Oro, taken there as gift for the god or to show to the priests who served him.

Birds were powerful emblems or 'shadows' of the gods in Polynesia. The shadow of 'Oro, for instance, was the frigate bird with its sinister winged silhouette. The shadow of Tane, by contrast, was a fabulous creature, a far-roaming red seabird which lived 'in the water of life'. A bird with folded wings carved from dark green serpentine must have seemed a mysterious but important object whose 'meaning' perhaps the priests of 'Oro could best interpret.

But why should an Asian vessel carrying a carved stone bird sail so far south in the first place? As it happened, towards the end of the thirteenth century, a tall window opened in China and attention was briefly turned to the southern hemisphere. There was a new emperor on the throne who had developed an interest in a marvellous bird rumoured to be living somewhere below the equator, and who is recorded as sending at least two expeditions 'to know and enquire' about it.

Chapter 17

'When the great lord has stayed ... three months in this city of Cambaluc ... he leaves ... in the month of March and goes into the country towards midday [south] as far as the Ocean-sea which is two days journey distant from the city. And he takes with him quite 10,000 falconers riding, and carries quite five hundred gerfalcons and peregrine falcons and saker falcons and other kinds of birds in great abundance for such are infinite and good in his domains, and they also carry goshawks in great quantity to catch birds on rivers.'[38]

These are the words of Marco Polo. The site of the palace of Cambaluc is now the centre of Beijing. Marco Polo arrived there, at the court of Kublai Khan, emperor of China, in about 1275, and he was back in Venice in 1295. He was not in fact the writer of his *Travels*, or *Marvels of the World*, or *The Description*, as it was variously entitled. The book is in the third person. Each chapter opens: 'Here he tells us of ...', the 'he' being Polo.

The writer was a man called Rustichello with whom Polo shared a prison cell for two years in Genoa, or who was possibly hired by the Genoese to go in and write down everything the prisoner told him. Whoever he was, he was fantastically prolix. Sentences curl round and round and nothing is stated without maddening care to keep, for example, subject and object and speaker and listener separate: 'And you may know quite truly that Master Marc stays with the Great Kaan quite seventeen years, and in all this time he did not cease to go on missions. For the great Kaan, since he sees that Master Marc so brought him back news from all parts and carried out well all the duties for which he sent him, for this reason all the important missions and the distant ones he gave all to Master Marc . . . Now this was the reason that Master Marc knows more of those things of that country than any other man, because he explores more of those strange regions than any man who was ever born; and also because he gave it his attention more to know this and to spy out and enquire what he might tell the great lord; whence it came about that there was never any who saw more lands than Master Marc . . .'

Polo was held in Genoa after being captured in a sea battle between Venetians and Genoese who were fighting for control of the eastern Mediterranean. He went to war in his own ship fitted out with a great catapult, a trebuchet, to sling stones at the Genoese and sink them, but instead ended up in a cell in a palace of red brick beside the sea in the enemy's capital.

He must have been a man of extraordinary charm. For years he was a kind of personal prisoner of the great Khan, who could not bear to let him go. In Genoa 'the fame of his rare qualities and his wonderful journey having spread abroad, all the city assembled to see and speak to him, treating him not as a prisoner but as a dear friend'.

Perhaps he got tired of repeating the stories of his travels and it was decided by gaolers and prisoner together to have them written down. The book was also known as *Il Milione*, either a reference to Polo's wealth or to the number of lies some people thought it contained. This scepticism has never entirely gone away but most scholars believe that Marco Polo did in fact go to China, stayed for a long time at the court of the great Khan, and later recorded accurately what he saw and heard, or thought he had heard.

'And the great lord always goes on two elephants or one, especially when he goes hawking, for the narrowness of the passes which are found in some places . . . but in his other doings he always goes on four elephants, on which he has a very beautiful wooden room, which is all covered inside with cloth of beaten gold and outside it is wrapped round and covered with lion skins, in which room the great Khan always stays when he goes hawking because he is troubled with gout . . .

'And several barons, twelve of his favourites with twelve women, stay there continually to make amusement and company for him. Round these elephants ride other barons who accompany the lord . . . When they see pheasants and cranes and other birds, they point them out to the falconers who are with the king and they immediately cry out . . . to him "Sir, cranes are passing," and the great lord immediately has the room uncovered above, then he sees the cranes and has those gerfalcons taken which he wishes, and lets them go after those cranes. And the gerfalcons often take the cranes and kill them before him, fighting with them for a long time, and it is a great amusement and delight to him.'

Elsewhere Polo describes other powerful beasts which Kublai Khan took hunting: 'You may know again that great Khan has indeed fierce animals with which he hunts, namely tame leopards all good at hunting with men, and many very large lions, much bigger than those of Babylonia. These are of very beautiful skin and of a very beautiful colour, for they are striped all over lengthwise in black and red and white . . . He also has a great multitude of eagles which are well trained to hunt, for they take wolves and foxes and buck and roe-deer, hares and other small animals. But those especially trained to catch wolves are extremely large and powerful, for you may know that there is no wolf so large as to get away from those eagles.'

At one point in *The Description*, Polo states that the great Khan sent at least two expeditions into the Southern Ocean in search of an even more powerful bird: 'You may know quite truly that in those islands . . . men who have gone there say that many very terrible grifon birds are found there. But yet you may know they are not made at all as our people believe . . . as half bird and half lion. But I tell you that I Marc, when I first heard this told, and asked those who said they had seen them, and those who have seen them asserted most constantly that they had no likeness of a beast in any part but have only two feet, like birds & they say that it is exactly like an eagle in shape but they say it is immeasurably great . . . And indeed it is true that . . . the great Khan Cublai sent his messengers there to know and enquire about the strange things of those islands, and again he sends word there to make them of this island release one of his messengers whom he sent to know about these things, but they have taken and held him captive ... That messenger of his brought to the lord, the great Khan, a feather of the wing of the said bird ruc.'

The islands where the 'said bird ruc' lived, Polo tells us, lay south of another much bigger island he names Mogedaxo and he is evidently talking about the country now called Madagascar, and repeating stories he heard in China, where it had been a fixed notion for at least a century that Madagascar was home to a huge bird known in China as the P'eng. This was not because an especially large eagle lived there but because Madagascar was or had once been the home of a huge flightless bird, *Aepyornis maximus*, larger even than the moa, and if *Aepyornis* was extinct by the Middle Ages, its great eggs and eggshells were still found from time to time, and the presence there of the P'eng followed by process of deduction.

The most authoritative Chinese treatises of the era, *Ling-wai-tai-ta* (*Answers from the Regions Beyond the Mountains*) of 1178, and *Chu-fan-chi* (*A Description of Barbarous Peoples*), written about 50 years later, give the same basic information: 'On this island there are usually great P'eng birds which so mask the sun that the shade on the sundial is shifted.'

Both books were written by officials in coastal cities of south China, where information about the outside world was more readily available than elsewhere in the country. *Ling-wai-tai-ta* makes it clear that the international sea trade at that time was almost entirely in the hands of foreigners. These visitors could be carefully questioned and their reports compared and collated, but even with most scrupulous care — and you sense that both these Chinese books were written by careful men — fantastic illusions creep in to their descriptions.

It is a pity, for instance, to realise there really never was such a place as Ch'a-pi-sha: 'The king wears a military robe with a golden girdle. On his head he wears a golden cap and on his feet black boots. His courtiers wear clothes embroidered with pearls. The people live in houses which are as much as seven storeys; on each storey lives a family. This country is resplendent with light for it is the place where the sun goes down. In the evening when the sun sets the sound of it is infinitely more terrifying than that of thunder, so every day a thousand men are placed at the gates who, as the sun goes down, mingle with the sound of the setting sun that of the blowing of horns and the beating of gongs and drums. If they did not do this, the women with child would hear the sound of the sun and would die of fright.'[39]

Marco Polo was caught up in this same web of uncertain marvels, and it is evident that while he was dictating or co-authoring his memoirs in Genoa he had no real idea of where Mogedaxo actually was. Almost none of the details he gives conform to Madagascan reality: 'The people of it are Saracens who worship the law of the abominable Mahomet . . . More elephants are bred on this island than in any other province in the world . . . Nothing is eaten in this island but elephants' flesh and camels' flesh. There are many very great trees of red sandal . . . and the finest ambergris . . . and many leopards and lynxes and bears and lions . . .'

Apart from the ambergris, which can drift to any shore in the world, and the sandalwood trees, which do in fact grow in Madagascar, none of this information applies to the great island in the south Indian Ocean, while much of it points clearly to the Horn of Africa. In short, Polo has confused the island with Mogadishu. (It is generally agreed today that Madagascar is called Madagascar only because Polo got it mixed up with Mogadishu, and the Portuguese, who reached the same island a few generations later, followed Polo's lead.)

But there are additional details in Polo's account of the expedition Kublai Khan sent into the Southern Ocean which are not found in *Ling-wai-tai-ta* and *Chu-fan-chi*, and which do not apply either to Mogadishu or Madagascar: 'This island is so far to the midday [south] that the ships cannot go sailing to other islands because the sea there runs so swiftly towards midday [south] that they would hardly be able to return back, and for this reason the ships do not go there . . . And again you may know that in those other islands which are in so great quantity towards midday where the ships as I said never go willingly for the current that runs in that region, men who have gone there say that those marvellous birds appeared there coming from towards midday at certain seasons of the year . . .'

This strong current running to the south is clearly a reference to the wei-lu, the whirlpool formed, according to Chinese mythology, above a drain in the sea floor which prevents the ocean from brimming over. Yet the wei-lu, which has the distinction of never existing *and* having a precise location, was always situated to the east and far to the south of China, in the Pacific. It was not something which mariners had to fear in the Indian Ocean. And nor are there myriad islands south of Madagascar.

It is possible that the wei-lu was added, for literary effect, to the story Polo heard, or that it was a standard formula for distant sea voyaging. We are in a world after all where Madagascar and the Horn of Africa can be easily confused, and where the sound of the setting sun is so terrifying in some places that trumpets are blown to drown it out. The seashell roar of fairy tales sounds in all directions.

As well as that, linguistic confusion must have reigned in the imperial court. Kublai Khan was Mongolian and he did not trust his Han Chinese subjects; many of his officials, like Polo, were foreigners, and it is not clear what language was used at court or if there was any common language at all. Polo is thought to have spoken and understood Persian and possibly Mongolian but not Chinese. His account of Mogedaxo and the terrible bird that lived nearby has elements of the game called 'Chinese whispers', with errors and guesswork creeping in at each retelling. But the details about the myriad islands and the wei-lu may also be based on fact, and point to a real expedition, an additional one perhaps, not to the Indian Ocean but into the Pacific.

The 'great Khan Cublai', who took 10,000 falconers with him and hunted with the fiercest animals he could find — tigers and eagles, for instance — could send ships anywhere he wanted. 'There is no man in the world who can find so great amusement and so great delight as he does, nor who has the power to do it,' says Polo. By the time the Khan ruled China, the story about the man from the Maghreb who sailed into the Pacific and saw the Rukh had been in circulation for at least a century and was well known in Baghdad and Persia, which both had become provinces of the Mongol empire, nominally ruled by Kublai Khan.

Ships capable of very distant expeditions were now available as well. A generation after Kublai Khan, Ibn Battuta saw huge Chinese vessels in port in southern India: 'On each of these ships serve a thousand men, of whom six hundred are sailors and four hundred are warriors. Amongst the latter are archers, shield-bearers and cross-bow archers . . . Four decks are constructed on the ship which contains apartments, cabins and rooms for the use of the merchants. The sailors let their children live in these quarters and they sow greenery, vegetables and ginger in wooden tubs. The administrator of the ship holds a position like that of a great emir. When he lands, the archers and the Abyssinians march before him with lances and swords, kettledrums, horns and trumpets. When he has reached his residence they plant their lances in the ground on both sides of his gate, and continue these ceremonies as long as he dwells there.'[40]

The soldiers were on board not only for grandeur, to 'project power' in the modern phrase, but also to protect the ship from marauders. To the writer of the *Chu-fan-chi*, all non-Chinese were more or less detestable, although he had a slightly better opinion of the people of Baghdad ('The inhabitants are tall and of a fine bright complexion, somewhat like the Chinese') and of the Iranians who lived on the slave-trading island of Kish ('The people of the country are white and clean and eight feet tall'), but the people in other countries such as Japan, Vietnam and Ceylon fare less well.[41]

Hearing that the kings of Japan formed an uninterrupted line of rulers, nevertheless 'the Emperor sighed and said "These are merely island barbarians."'[42] But at least the Japanese had a king and a criminal code, made war according to the proprieties and stood in awe of (Chinese) civilisation. The savage seafolk, the 'black slave devils' as the Chinese called the indigenous races of Southeast Asia and beyond, brought only horror to the Chinese mind, although in southern Chinese cities it was also a fashion, borrowed from the Arabs, to keep black slaves as gatekeepers. Some of these were African but many were from the Negrito population, the aboriginal peoples of Asia.

In 1370 'little foreign slaves' were among the gifts to the court of China brought by an embassy from Malacca. A king of Java sent 300 more in 1381. 'In Kuang-chou,' another writer, P'ing-chou-k'o-t'an, tells us, 'rich people keep many devil slaves . . . also called wild people . . . black in colour, as black as ink . . . they are natives of islands beyond the sea of China. They live (in their native land) on raw food. When caught and fed on food with fire it purges them daily . . . During this treatment many die but if they do not they may be reared and become able to understand human speech [Chinese] although they cannot learn to speak it.'[43]

Trade with these peoples in their own land was possible only as speechless barter. In the Philippines, as we saw earlier, the indigenous people 'lurk in the jungle and shoot arrows at passers-by unseen. If thrown a porcelain bowl, they will stoop and pick it up and go away leaping and shouting for joy.' In Palawan, two inhabitants would be taken as hostages while negotiations took place. You held up one object and pointed to another. More complex communication was thought to be impossible. One thing was plain to the writer of *Chu-fan-chi*: 'The farther one penetrates among these islands, the worse the robbers are.'

If expeditions 'to know and enquire' about the Rukh were to be sent among such people, precautions would be necessary. First, there was the matter of security; shield-bearers and crossbow archers on board could provide that. Then there was the question of communication. The seafolk might have useful information but they did not understand 'human' speech. The dumb-show of barter would be of no use here. It would be a precise and rather abstruse question that needed answering. Where, in the vastness of the ocean, in which direction, was the place where the P'eng lived?

This is the moment when a visual aid of some kind might be useful. Could a compact representation, weighing about 2 kilograms, of a strange bird with clawed feet, carved in dark green serpentine, have been taken on an expedition below the equator as a translator's tool?

The immediate objection to this theory is that the Korotangi, whatever it represents, does not look like an eagle and has never been taken for one. On the other hand, as we saw, the appearance of the mythical birds of Asia was unstable. They changed from place to place and over time. In India, Garuda began as a fiery eagle, was transformed into a large white parrot and then into other avian species before settling again on an aquiline form, although this time with a man's face and a flabby belly. In his journey west, to Persia and Arabia, Garuda became the Rukh, which took on its own identity but also adopted the same appearances as the Anqa and the Simurgh, which were themselves subject to change.

Garuda also went east, first as the chariot of the Hindu god Vishnu, and then as protector of the Buddha and chariot of the bodhisattva. Across south and east Asia today it is a fundamentally Hindu monster which guards Buddhist temples and palace gates, although while travelling east Garuda continued to change, becoming more avian and acquiring a beak again instead of a mouth and nose.

But when he reached China, something quite different happened. China had a venerable mythical aviary of its own, and the Indian bird-man type did not settle in easily. Although Garuda kept the aquiline form in Buddhist temples where Tibetan (and later Mongolian) influence was strong, and while one ancient Chinese weather god, Sire Thunder, began to take on Garuda-like characteristics (clawed feet, a beak) Garuda was for the most part identified with one of China's own legendary birds, the P'eng. Could the Korotangi then be a representation of the ancient Chinese being, the fabulous P'eng?

The difficulty here is that the P'eng is rarely represented in art, or only obliquely — as part of a wing for instance, seen here in a later Japanese print.

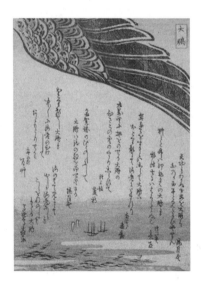

Even in very early references, the P'eng seems to have been too huge and cloudy to paint or render in stone. In the fourth century BCE, for instance, Master Zhuang wrote that in the northern ocean lived a fish called K'un and every six months K'un changed into the bird P'eng and rose high above the Earth on a whirlwind 'like the whorls of a goat's horn' and began a journey towards the south and the sun. 'When P'eng journeys to the Southern Ocean, he mounts 90,000 miles, nor does he cease flying for six months without stopping. Is the azure of the sky its true colour or is it the colour of infinity? When the bird looks down, everything looks the same as above, all is lost in a haze, a dust-storm, a cloud left by an army of horsemen. It is only then when he is 90,000 miles high, with the wind underneath him, that P'eng rests on the wind and with the blue sky on his back sets his course for the South.'

A Ming dynasty encyclopedia has this to say: 'It is possible to find the sizes of all things in the universe — except the K'un which is transformed into the P'eng. [Master Zhuang] refers to it at the beginning of his writings. However it is a little difficult to believe in.'[44]

K'un and P'eng are a pair in the yin-yang system which divides natural phenomena into opposites — bright and dark, wet and dry, aerial and aquatic, male and female — which are all also slowly interchanging. The system is much older than the fourth century BCE[45] and the legend of the P'eng flying towards the light is probably older still, deriving from the sight of geese and cranes flying south in autumn, one of those phenomena which move us with a strange form of nostalgia — a longing for the world as it still in fact is.

By the fourth century BCE, the fabulous P'eng was

appearing in rather obvious Taoist parables: 'The cicada and the little dove laugh at the great P'eng, saying: "We set off with a hop and a jump to the nearest hedge, which is good enough for us. What's all this fuss about rising 90,000 miles in order to fly south?"

'The understanding of little creatures cannot be compared to that of the great. The cicada has no comprehension even of the autumn, for he lives but a moment.'

By the Middle Ages, P'eng had become a simple symbol of aspiration and achievement in China. 'Shen Hui, passing through Tianchang on his way to attend the metropolitan exam, dreamed he rode on the back of P'eng bird which soared up in the wind . . . And during the Xuanhe period of the Song dynasty he indeed became top graduate in China.'

Yet what did P'eng *look* like? The sources are vague, but a real, early, and earthly origin can be glimpsed. Swans and geese, for instance, were like P'eng and definitively yang. 'The wild goose is said to be peculiarly the bird of the yang, or the principle of light or masculinity. It follows the sun in its course to the south and shows an instinctive knowledge of the times and the seasons . . . The wild swan is considered a larger congener of the wild goose which it is said to accompany on its flight.'[46]

An ancient Han-dynasty divination manual makes the same point:

> The sounds of geese. An impressive sight!
> They rise up high, and transform like spirits.
> Turning their backs on darkness they face the light,
> Through the Tao, they are blessed and meritorious

In an eighth-century poem, 'Rhapsody to the P'eng' by Li Bai, the mythical bird is overtly linked to a real swan:

> When P'eng breathes out, clouds are born in the Six
> Conjunctions,
> When it moults feathers, snow flies for a thousand
> miles ...
> How compare it to even the yellow swan of P'eng-lai,
> Flaunting golden jacket with chrysanthemum skirt?[47]

The 'yellow swan of Peng-lai' was a well-known reference: 'In 86 BC, the first year of the Shih-yuan period of the Former Han, an auspicious yellow swan descended to the Grand Liquor Pool north of the Palace of Established Blazonry.' The emperor composed a celebratory song of the event, which included the line 'Gold makes its jacket, oh, chrysanthemum makes its skirt.'

The Grand Liquor Pool in the palace garden contained three rocks which represented the Isles of Immortality, located somewhere in the sea east of China. In ancient times they were not thought to be very far away. The first Qin emperor, Qin Shi Huang (259–210 BCE), sent ships in search of them, and the Han emperor Wu Ti (141–87 BCE) even went down to the coast to see if he couldn't spy them out himself from the beach.

Over time, as naval technology improved, the Isles of Immortality naturally retreated further and further into the distance and finally became the destination of P'eng itself on his annual journey south. When a real swan landed with a splash in the garden pool with the three rocks it was seen as an envoy from the Immortals, a fabulous but minor P'eng with real, wet feathers.

Much later, in the Song dynasty, we are told that the P'eng

was actually reborn in human form, as a certain Yo Fei, who became famous as 'a protector spirit of small rural places' and whose titles included 'Yo' and also the 'King of O'. At his birth, as clear evidence of his P'eng-ness, 'a large bird like a swan flew over the house, and screamed, giving him the name *Fei* . . .'

If, in thirteenth-century China, a commission came from on high, even from the palace of Kublai Khan himself, for an image to be made, a carving in stone, of the P'eng, which might be useful on an expedition into the lands of the wild sea-people, this would pose a problem for a sculptor: *Clouds are born in the Six Conjunctions, When [the P'eng] moults feathers, snow flies for a thousand miles . . .* A Chinese workshop might well turn to something more manageable, a creature of flesh and blood, extremely yang, and still seen passing high above in the autumn sky — namely a swan or goose, or perhaps the Chinese swan-goose, which was known to soar to great heights, was also a symbol of aspiration and, with its high and almost vertical frontal bone, in fact rather resembles the Korotangi.

Is the Korotangi, therefore, a representation of China's P'eng taking the form of a swan-goose? The idea is highly provisional, depending on a whole series of 'ifs', and if just one fails, the whole structure falls. First, Marco Polo would have to have been right in saying that Kublai Khan sent expeditions to search or enquire about the griffin; second, he would have to be wrong to tell us that ships went only to Mogadexo in the Indian Ocean; third, an image of a bird would have had to be made and taken on the voyage; fourth, it must represent not the Rukh or Garuda in their Arab or Indian forms, but the P'eng, in the form of a traditional yang species; fifth, this object would have to be carried into the South Pacific and its ownership transferred, either peacefully or violently, to Polynesians living on one of the many hundreds of islands they inhabited; sixth, this must have then been taken to the sacred island of Raiatea; and seventh, it must have then been given into the possession of people who afterwards sailed on the Tainui canoe to the very country where the original object of the expedition — the real eagle, that is — happened to be living.

Together, it was all rather difficult to believe, and yet weighed against this excessive cloudiness is a single hard fact: one morning in 1878 a bird of dark green serpentine was found under the roots of a tree 11,000 kilometres from its apparent place of manufacture, and no one knows why.

Is the carving, then, solid evidence of the kind Professor Bivar would have liked to see as proof that voyages into the South Pacific and a sighting of *Harpagornis* were behind the mediaeval legend of the Rukh? It can hardly be said to be proof, since real proof is hard to imagine in this context, and so we are left only with theory. And there is the famous problem of theory: 'No theory fits all the facts because we never know all the facts.' My theory fitted a few known facts, but what about all the rest, the innumerable unknown facts?

Je n'y crois pas. This phrase came into my mind. 'I don't believe it.'

Why the thought came to me in French, I don't know; I wasn't even sure whose thought it was. Was it mine, or some imagined reader or critic? In any case it seemed wise to agree. I didn't really believe my own theory, or not as it stood. But that led straight back to the mystery of the object among the roots of the mānuka tree, or, in my case, on the landing of the stairs of the old museum at Buckle Street.[48] *Over how many miles of ocean have those stone wings flown?*

The question charmed me at the time, and gave me an excuse not to worry much about my complete lack of interest in the puzzles of torts and contract law. The question was still there, and I still had a feeling that the carving had something important to reveal. A theory may fail but its subject doesn't go away. The only thing to do was to go in search of more facts.

The Korotangi did not arrive in the daylight of 1878 as an impenetrable mystery. It readily gave up some of its history — it had been made with metal tools, for instance, and the design of the feathers pointed to an east Asian workshop. But it came with something more important. It came with a name.

In fact it had three names: Korota, Korotau and Korotangi. Ingenious efforts have been made to deconstruct these words, breaking them into constituent Māori parts, 'koro' and 'tangi' being the most obvious, although without compelling results. Koro is best known as an affectionate term for an old man. Tangi indicates sorrow, weeping, bereavement. Separately or together they don't seem to have much to do with a carved stone bird, its head stretched forward as if about to take flight.

There is another possibility. Perhaps korotangi is not a Māori word at all but a foreign name with a Māori cloak thrown over it. There are no strict rules that apply when a new word enters a language. Some remain strictly exotic but most of them acquire some camouflage to let them fit in better, hide their immigrant status. Thousands of loan-words have come into English and undergone these changes and the principle is universal, which can be seen clearly when the same word or name goes into several different languages. The word garuda, for instance, which made its way right across India and out into the wider world, adjusted in different ways in new habitats:

Sanskrit: garuda
Pali: garula
Tamil: karutan
Burmese: galone
Thai: khrut
Mongolian: khangarid
Japanese: karura

In Burmese, the 'r' and 'd' are replaced by a more liquid 'l' and 'n'. In Thai, three full syllables are compacted to one. In Mongolian, a stern expansion and contraction have taken place at the same time. Looking at this list, I wondered what would happen to garuda if it came into the Polynesian language area.

But before I could take the thought any further, the Tamil version, karutan, seemed to jump from the page. I remembered reading that Kublai Khan held the Tamils in high estimation. Their maritime kingdom in southern India was wealthy and powerful — the 'richest in existence' said

Marco Polo — and the great Khan worshipped success. Not trusting his Han Chinese subjects, he promoted Tamils to 'key government, military and diplomatic posts'[49] and went to the trouble of building them a Shiva temple in southern China. When or if he sent out the expeditions that Marco Polo mentions, to 'know and enquire' about a mighty hunting bird, it is quite possible that he would commission Tamils for the task, and that a Tamil vessel would set sail. In that case, the name of the bird being looked for below the equator would not be P'eng, or Rukh, or Garuda, but Karutan.

What would become of karutan making its entry into a Polynesian language? The first thing it would do is change its shape. Tahitian and Māori are allergic to consonantal endings. Dozens of English words had to be improved when they arrived in Māori in the eighteenth and nineteenth century — king became kingi, queen kuini, book puka, sheep hipi, street tiriti, sixpence hiccapenny and so on. According to this rule, karutan might either drop the 'n' — karuta — or acquire an additional vowel.

The acclimatisation process would not yet be over. Loan words often drift towards familiar sounds or associations. Karu does exist as a Māori word — the eye — but koro is much more common. There are ten words that begin with karu in my Māori dictionary and eight pages of koro. The karu of karutan, arriving into Māori, could easily edge towards koro and then the name would be well on its way to korota or korotau, with korotangi bringing up the rear. Korotangi is now the best-known name of the carving: the rhythm is good, and tangi is a core word in Māori, with a host of meanings as a verb — to cry, shout, coo, roar, make a loud noise, sound like the sea;

while as a noun it has a central role in Māori culture, being the name for mourning and the funeral rites.

Phonetic coincidence is a poor basis on which to build a theory but may reasonably be used to support one. Was korotangi a Māori version of the Tamil karutan? Were the names in the song sung over the carving a final indication that Professor Bivar was right? Again it could not be described as proof — we are back in the cloudiness of language — but, for my part, when I first saw the three syllables, *ka*, *ru* and *tan* they seemed to lift off the page and fly to korota, korotau and korotangi, and I had the sense that I had just come in sight of the end of the journey, glimpsed in the Rare Books Room and then by the third of the three arches across the Ōpārara River, a journey which, in fact, led me through the records and legends of several civilisations, and halfway around the world.

For if karutan really was the source of korotangi, then several questions could be answered with some confidence. First, the subject of the carving could be made out. It is a representation, probably in Chinese form, of Garuda, the winged master-spirit of south Asian mythology, with certain family ties to the Rukh, the Anqa and the Simurgh of the Middle East.

The carving's presence in New Zealand, secondly, suggests Professor Bivar was right when he argued that there had been at least one visit by an Arab or south Asian vessel to the then-unnamed land, and that the existence of a great eagle in the South Seas was subsequently known in Asia, for even Kublai Khan with all the resources at his command would not have despatched an expedition to that remote region without a reason.

It is possible to imagine the scenario: a ship is commissioned to go in search of a huge raptorial bird rumoured to exist there. The ship anchors off an atoll or high island in Polynesia. There is cautious, anxious contact between the crew and the local people, sounding out one another's strength and disposition. At some point a pleasing object is produced and the word karutan is heard. Perhaps everything passes off peacefully. Perhaps some pilfering takes place, as it usually did on first contact, by both sides. Perhaps there is a fight — some of the crew are taken prisoner, as Marco Polo states, and even killed.

Or perhaps the object actually serves as a translator's aid and a local navigator comes aboard — Tahitians and New Zealand Māori often sailed away on the first European ships they ever saw — and the vessel goes on in the right direction and even reaches the South Island, where *Harpagornis* is glimpsed. Marco Polo was definite that his informants, or their sources, saw the 'grifons' with their own eyes. 'Those who have seen them asserted most constantly that . . . it is exactly like an eagle in shape but they say it is immeasurably strong.'

And then, thirdly — and this was the clearest conclusion of all, and it doesn't rely on Professor Bivar or the Rukh or Garuda or the Korotangi, although they point in the same direction — we can now see the real symbolic value, the deep 'meaning' of the great eagle of the South Seas which, it seemed to me when I read about it in 2009, had been left out of the ecosystem of symbols, on the world stage at least.

In the Māori tradition, as we saw, Te Hōkioi stood for power, danger and the sublime — the normal attributes of eagles elsewhere, but this eagle, the largest of all and last to be encountered, had one unique symbolic value. The trouble was that no one who ever saw it, least of all the first navigators to the region, Polynesians perhaps as early as the sixth or seventh centuries, or — possibly — Arab or Persian sailors in the eleventh century, knew or could possibly have known what was really happening when they reached the unknown land. At that moment they were completing the final stage of one of mankind's greatest achievements — the exploration of an empty planet.

The process had begun long ago, it is generally agreed, in Africa, and once people left Africa it took another 100,000 years. It was a journey about which we know almost nothing. There must have been, for instance, a first small band of *Homo sapiens* to stand on a hill and look out over the forests, say, of France, or to set foot on the Gangetic Plain, or call out in a river valley in China, but those things took place far too long ago for the faintest recollection to survive. Even entry into the Americas was over 20,000 years ago and too distant for any trace in the records of transmitted memory.

But the final chapter of the exploration, in the South Pacific, was only about a thousand or perhaps 1500 years ago, and there, in the south-west corner, waiting for them, so to speak, on the very last page, a great eagle rose in the air to mark the occasion — dangerous, beautiful, itself now doomed, a symbol of final achievement, and of ignorance (since none of them knew what was really happening) and yet also of knowledge, for without an eagle rushing down on Rata as in the Tahiti legend or the man from the Maghreb as in the Arab stories, like a furious secretary — 'you won't forget *me* in a hurry' — we would never know, and scholars such as Bivar would have no reason to speculate, that such early journeys took place.

And since there are no other records of the 100,000-year-long exploration, those from the South Pacific must stand for the entire process. Through them we have a picture of the world as it was before human beings arrived. These last stories are surprisingly detailed. We know what people saw and said and thought. Here, for example, is an account of the exact moment that Kupe, one of the earliest Polynesian travellers, first saw the South Island. He had been circumnavigating the North Island and stopped to catch fish one day on the southern coast.

After he stopped, clouds further south must have lifted: 'Raising his eyes, [Kupe] saw over the sea the mountains of the South Island, the snows of Tapuae-nuku in the sun. Hineuira, one of his daughters, asked Kupe what he was gazing at.

'He replied, "It is nothing; I was looking at the shoals of fish coming in when I lifted my eyes and saw the land lying there."

'Hineuira said "Let the name of these stones be Matakitaki," which remains to this day.'[50]

Matakitaki means to gaze, to look fixedly and keep looking, and it is still there on the map, Matakitaki, about 80 kilometres from Wellington, where Kupe and Hineuira stood looking at the Kaikōura mountains 100 kilometres across the sea, without any idea that just then they were completing a great silvery loop in human knowledge. The last habitable land on Earth had been seen.

There are many Māori accounts of this kind, which differ in different tribal traditions but give us an impression of the whole world as it was — still, shining, silent, uncanny:

'Rakataura was the first man who came to Aotearoa. He looked for the fires of the inhabitants, but could not see any . . . He returned to Hawaiki and said "I have been to a land where no man lives nor fire is seen."

'Tamatea sailed all round New Zealand . . . At the entrance to every inlet, he waited and listened for any sound . . . Off the mouth of the Arahura River he heard voices . . . but did not discover his wives, being unable to recognise them in the enchanted stones over which its waters murmured.

'Kupe . . . was the first man to land on these islands. He went . . . to Patea where he heard the cry of the kokako inland . . . and he thought it was the voice of man, and he went to see the man who had uttered that voice, but he did not see any man.

'We called inland, but no one answered.'[51]

No one answered.

There, in three words, is the whole history of the human race for many millennia, as people made their way through an empty world.

I thought of that silence the day I heard that my friend Jim Vivieaere had died. I was living in Wellington at the time; I had a writer's residency on the lower slopes of what used to be called Mount Tinakori — Mount Nothing-for-Dinner — but the house was in a steep valley and in winter it was rather dark. The sun struck the front windows for a minute or two, peered into the kitchen ten minutes later and then was off for the rest of the day, and I got into the habit of chasing it, of going out and climbing the hill, which now had its old name back, Te Ahumairangi, which contains the sense of 'whirlwind', or later in the day driving over to the eastern or southern suburbs to walk along the beaches which were still in the sun.

I was going out the front door one morning when my phone buzzed. It was a text from a friend in Auckland. 'Jim taken to hospital in ambulance.' I was surprised at this. I knew he had been very ill — he had been diagnosed with liver cancer a few months before — but that week we heard he was feeling much better and that he himself thought the disease was in remission; his daughter Cypress, who had been looking after him, then took a week off and flew to Melbourne for a break.

Half an hour later, as I was climbing up the hill to the first ridge where the sunlight was waiting, my phone buzzed again. I stopped on a muddy path in the shadow.

'Jim passed just now at Auckland Hospital.'

'*Passed*?' I thought stupidly — then the 'away' came, and since there was nothing else to do, I carried on walking up into the sunlight and this time I went right to the top of the hill and came out on a paddock of rough grass surrounded by pines, and looking south I saw the snow-capped Kaikōuras across the sea. The South Island is not always visible from Wellington, and those particular mountains, the Kaikōuras, had a special connotation for me. It was there that for the first, and so far only, time in my life, I heard an unusual natural phenomenon: utter silence.

This is far less common than you might think. Wherever you are outside there is usually something — wind, waves, traffic, a dog barking, rain, birdsong, music from a builder's radio — to interrupt the deep background silence of the

Earth turning on what Milton called *her soft axle*. But on that occasion, when we were driving down to Christchurch and passing the Kaikōuras, we left the highway and took a road up the Clarence Valley to see what was there and after a few miles we stopped, got out of the car, stood on the side of the hill and looked inland. And there was . . . no sound.

There was a wind blowing because I could see cloud-shadows racing over higher inland slopes, but the wind was too high to be heard and not a leaf or grass stem was moving nearby; there was a river across the flats but it was too far away to be heard, and by chance there were no birds calling or dogs barking or aircraft overhead and no one else was on the road, and the absence of sound in the Clarence Valley just then was so intense that a special word seemed to come along for it.

Interstellar.

This is the silence which pertains among the stars.

Later that week in Christchurch I happened to read an account of the Waitaha people reaching the South Island. They were the first people to settle there and before going ashore they circumnavigated the island in the canoe *Uruao*, looking for signs of inhabitants and finally coming ashore near the Kaikōuras. They were ones who 'called inland, but no one answered'.[52] The inland mountains, which I saw with the cloud shadows racing over them, are still named Ka Whata Tu o Rakihouia, the Storehouse of Rakihouia, after the son of the captain of the canoe.

This was not far down the coast from the place where in 1948 a complete eagle skeleton was found and then left behind in an old iron oven, and it was the Waitaha who also left us the most detailed description of a battle with a great eagle, on Tāwera, so it cannot have been long before they heard the whistle of pinions and realised that they were not alone in the new land.

But I wasn't thinking about the eagle at that time, and when I read the story of the Waitaha and their first landfall it occurred to me that the hush I had heard in the Clarence Valley a few days before was not just the absence of noise but a kind of echo, a memory, there among the mountains, in the last place to be discovered by human beings, of the great silence which once hung over the whole world.

Of course I knew this was just a fancy and that silences don't leave echoes and mountains don't have memories but all the same, standing on the top of Te Ahumairangi on the day Jim died and looking at the Kaikōuras across the sea, I thought of my old friend who that morning had ended his journey through the world, and I thought of the Waitaha standing on the unknown shore, *listening.*

Notes

I

1 All transcripts of the inquest and press commentary are from *Lyttelton Times*, 21 March 1860.

2 H. F. von Haast, *The Life & Times of Julius Von Haast: A New Zealand Pioneer* (1948), 487.

3 Ibid.

4 *Transactions and Proceedings of the Royal Society of New Zealand*, vol. 3 (1871), 192.

5 Elsdon Best, *Forest Lore of the Maori* (Wellington: Te Papa Press, 2005 [1942]), 166.

6 Julius von Haast, *Geology of the Provinces of Canterbury and Westland, New Zealand* (Christchurch: The Times, 1879), 37 and 135.

7 There is an island in the Ionian Sea which Homer named Taphos, on account of its sea caves. One is so large that a Greek submarine used to hide there in the Second World War.

8 Trevor H. Worthy, *Fossils of Honeycomb Hill* (Wellington: Museum of New Zealand Te Papa Tongarewa, 1993), 13.

9 Unpublished report on a visit to Honeycomb Hill Caves, National Museum of New Zealand, 12 August 1982.

10 Trevor Worthy and Richard Holdaway, *The Lost World of the Moa: Prehistoric Life of New Zealand* (Christchurch: Canterbury University Press, 2002), 286.

11 As a result of this discovery, *Harpagornis*'s name was officially changed to *Hieraaetus moorei*, and then to *Aquila moorei*, and then back to *Hieraaetus moorei*. Since it might change again, and also to conserve Haast's fine analogy of the grappling hook, the name *Harpagornis* might still appear in this book.

12 Sibling eagle chicks can breed, but only if the parents themselves are not closely related.

13 Michael Bunce et al., 'Ancient DNA provides new insights into the evolutionary history of New Zealand's extinct giant eagle', *PLOS Biology* 3, no. 1 (2005).

14 This and the following three quotes are from R. Paul Scofield and Ken W. S. Ashwell, 'Rapid somatic expansion causes the brain to lag behind: The case of the brain and behavior of New Zealand's Haast's Eagle', *Journal of Vertebrate Paleontology* 29, no. 3 (2009): 637–49.

15 'Methinks I see in my mind a strong and puissant nation . . . an eagle mewing her mighty youth' — this was England as seen by Milton in 1664, in *Areopagitica*.

16 Philippe Sands, *Torture Team: Rumsfeld's Memo and the Betrayal of American Values* (New York: St Martin's Press, 2008).

17 Worthy, *Fossils of Honeycomb Hill*.

II

1 James West Stack, *South Island Maoris: A Sketch of Their History and Legendary Lore* (Christchurch: Whitcombe & Tombs, 1898), 26.

2 Herries Beattie, *Maori Place-Names of Canterbury: Including One Thousand Hitherto Unpublished Names Collected from Maori Sources*, 2nd edn (Dunedin: *Otago Daily Times*, 1945), 91.

3 Herries Beattie, *Traditional Lifeways of the Southern Maori: The Otago University Museum Ethnological Project, 1920*, ed. Atholl Anderson (Dunedin: Otago University Press/Otago Museum, 1994), 339.

4 Stack, *South Island Maoris*.

5 Peter Maling (ed.), *The Torlesse Papers* (Christchurch: Pegasus Press, 1958), 195.

6 Harry Evison, *The Long Dispute: Maori Land Rights and European Colonisation in Southern New Zealand* (Christchurch: Canterbury University Press, 1997), 196.

7 Mantell's report to Lt-Governor Eyre was printed in the *Appendix to the Journals of the House of Representatives* in 1858. All the Mantell quotations in this chapter are from his diary or from his sketchbook, both held in the Alexander Turnbull Library, Wellington. There is also a typescript of the diary, although this has been edited and differs here and there from the original. In fact a haze of unreliability hangs over all the Mantell sources. The diary was clearly written up later, presumably to concur with his official report, which made light of Māori opposition to Mantell's egregious decisions.

8 *Transactions and Proceedings of the Royal Society of New Zealand* (1872), 94.

9 Evison, *The Long Dispute*, 169.

10 John White, *The Ancient History of the Maori, His Mythology and Traditions*, vol. 3 (1887–1890), 253.

11 See Byron, *Don Juan*, vol. XI, 135.

12 This is attributed to Einstein.

13 National Archives, Wellington, in Eyre-Grey 21.6.49, NAW G7/6. no. 62.

14 Ibid.

15 Maling, *The Torlesse Papers*, 122.

16 *The Spectator*, vol. 20 (1847): 1070.

17 Letter XXIV, *Godley's Letters from America* (1844), 204ff.

18 Maling, *The Torlesse Papers*, 184.

19 The reports of this excursion are taken from Maling, *The Torlesse Papers*; Charlotte Godley, *Letters from Early New Zealand,* ed. John Godley (Christchurch: Whitcombe & Tombs, 1951); 'Pilgrim days in Canterbury — Notes from an unpublished diary: Impressions of E. J. Wakefield specially written for "The Press"', Christchurch *Press*, 16 December 1909.

20 *Globe,* 10 May 1879.

21 *Lyttelton Times,* 8 May 1879.

22 Te Maire Tau, 'Property rights in Kaiapoi', *VUW Law Review* 47, no. 4 (2016): 684.

23 *Lyttelton Times,* 10 May 1879.

24 *Lyttelton Times,* 19 May 1879.

25 Te Uki, reported in Christchurch *Press*, 14 May 1879; *Lyttelton Times,* 15 May 1879.

26 Ngāi Tahu Claims Settlement Act 1998.

27 Evison, *The Long Dispute*, 303.

28 Godley, *Letters from Early New Zealand.*

29 The plans for Christchurch were very carefully considered, down to the most minor details. Yet a footnote to one of Torlesse's diary entries reveals that the entire establishment of the city was the purest chance. After looking around for nearly three weeks the chief surveyor, Captain Thomas, decided it might not be the best place for 'Canterbury' after all, and other locations should be examined: 'Accordingly the bows of the little cutter *Fly* were turned to the southward but she refused to move. A strong sou-wester had suddenly sprung up. They tried again a little later, but the same thing happened. Captain Thomas accepted the omen. "Here," he said, "let us stay. The fates are against us. These shall be the Canterbury Plains."' (Maling, *The Torlesse Papers*, 54, footnote).

But for that puff of wind Christchurch would not have been built where it was and much of what is outlined in this book would never have taken place. By then Mantell had already robbed Ngāi Tahu of their land and Metehau had run at him with an axe, so that story would have continued, although in ways we cannot see, but otherwise — no Glenmark, no Haast holding up a great claw in front of the Christchurch Philosophical Society, no Canterbury Museum, no city falling down in a cloud of dust one day in 2011, and while books would be written on the eagle, they wouldn't include this one since the writer would not exist — his parents, two grandparents and possibly two great-grandparents all having first met in the little town which was photographed from the spire of the cathedral, about 30 years after a gale arrested the bows of the little cutter *Fly*.

III

1   Hamdullah al-Mustaufi al-Qazwini, The Zoological Section of *Nuzhatu-I-Qulûb*, 740 AH (1340 CE), trans. J. Stephenson (1928), 80.

2   Ibid.

3   All quotes from al-Jahiz are taken from *Life and Work of Jahiz*, trans. Charles Pellat (London: D. M. Hawke, 1965).

4   Baldassare Castiglione, *The Book of the Courtier* (1528). Castiglione is neglected today, more people preferring to take advice from Machiavelli, who wrote *The Prince* about the same time as Castiglione wrote *The Courtier*, and who took exactly the opposite position on politics and ethics.

5   The Ducal Palace is still there and you can go and stand at the same window, although not at a dawn the colour of a rose, since the palace is now an art gallery and doesn't open until 8.30 am.

6   Joseph Banks, *The Endeavour Journal of Joseph Banks*, vol. 1, 17 January 1770.

7   Teuira Henry, *Ancient Tahiti*, Bernice P. Bishop Museum, Bulletin 48, Honolulu (1928), 495.

8   Tane Watere Te Kahu (Ngāi Tahu) quoted in S. Percy Smith, *Hawaiki: The Original Home of the Maori* (Christchurch: Whitcombe & Tombs, 1904), 47.

9   *Journal of the Polynesian Society* 19, no. 4 (1910): 176.

10 *Journal of the Polynesian Society* 19, no. 3 (1910): 142.

11 Henry, *Ancient Tahiti*, 495.

12 Banks, *The Endeavour Journal*, 452.

13 John Wilson, 'Mt Taranaki in Cook's journal', *Te Ara — The Encyclopedia of New Zealand*: www.TeAra.govt.nz/en/photograph/3934/mt-taranaki-in-cooks-journal-13-january-1770

14   One objection to the idea that Taranaki is the great landmark of Hiti
      Marama in these tales is the scientific consensus that the Pouākai never
      lived in the North Island, the evidence being that no eagle remains have
      ever been found there. This ignores evidence of another kind — Māori
      place-names, for example. The range of hills adjacent to Mount Taranaki
      is *named* Pouākai, and a nearby coastal settlement of Pungarehu has the
      same name as the hero in one of the tales about the 'demon bird'. And it
      seems likely that one eagle bone has been found in Taranaki, in the cache
      of fossils stolen by Walter Mantell. It was not identified at the time, and
      scientists argue it must have been inadvertently mixed up with other
      bones Mantell sent to England, by which time he had searched known
      eagle habitat in the South Island. Yet Mantell shipped off the Taranaki
      fossils in 1846, well before he set foot in the south. The puzzle is probably
      insoluble now, but it seems wonderfully apt that the 'Extinguisher', who
      caused such misery and confusion in the South Island, also, through
      theft and ambition, caused this little scientific mystery which remains.
      If he had left the Taranaki bones where they were, for the real owner
      to come back with a horse and cart to collect, we would now know for
      certain whether the fossil was among them, and have a better idea if
      the eagle ever flew in Taranaki skies. But it doesn't seem unlikely that
      Harpagornis, whose ancestors once flew across the Tasman, might from
      time to time have crossed the sea to the North Island and established
      itself on the opposite coast.

15   'Nukuroa' and 'Nukutaira' are also given as very early Māori names for
      New Zealand by John White in *The Ancient History of the Maori*, vol. 8
      (1887–1890), 105, 136.

16   White, *The Ancient History of the Maori*, vol. 1 (1887–1890), 91; and vol.
      3, 2–4.

17   There is a cave named named Matuku-takotako on Cashmere hill
      in Christchurch, and the nearby beach of Sumner was also named
      Matuku-takotako before English settlers arrived and renamed it after the
      Archbishop of Canterbury. Nearby is another cave where an eagle bone,
      fashioned into an awl, was found. The appearance of the ancient name of
      the ogre of the Polynesian tales so close to known eagle habitat brings the
      Polynesian legends of Hiti Marama even closer to New Zealand. See W. A.
      Taylor, *Lore and History of the South Island Maori* (Christchurch, 1952), 49.

18   White, *The Ancient History of the Maori*, vol. 2 (1887–1890), 33.

19   In later mythology Matuku dwindles into the form of a bittern, matuku-
      hūrepo, shy, rarely seen, quite harmless, but with a mysterious booming
      call.

20   Most of the information about these enchanted beings comes from
      Elsdon Best's *Maori Religion and Mythology Part 2* (Wellington: A. R.
      Shearer, 1982).

21   Hamiora Pio (Ngāti Awa) in *Journal of the Polynesian Society* 10, no. 4 (December 1901). Kite flying was a semi-sacred pastime: the whole community would gather to watch, and call out this chant as the kite ascended to its ancestor, Te Hōkioi. Only high chiefs were permitted to handle and fly the kite itself. The oldest kite in existence is owned by the British Museum but when I saw it, it was in a drawer in a museum storeroom in the back streets of north London — a strange dark prison for the 'offspring' of Te Hōkioi who lived in the Eighth Heaven.

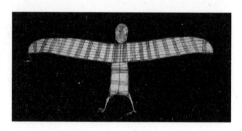

22   Elsdon Best, *Maori Religion and Mythology Part 2*, 563. There is some debate about the origin of this chant. It may be very ancient, dating from the time when a fourteenth-century observer saw an eagle overhead, or it may have been coined in the 1820s in the powerful mind of the chief Te Rauparaha, who sent a message in this form to his allies warning them of an attack being planned by their tribal enemies. In the 1860s, a Māori newspaper was set up and named *Te Hokioi* specifically to warn of war with European settlers, which duly broke out.

23   Best, *Maori Religion and Mythology Part 2*, 563.

24   Fa-hsien, *A Record of Buddhistic Kingdoms*, quoted in the introduction to an English translation of *Chu-fan-chi: A Description of Barbarian Peoples* by Ju-kua Chao (St Petersburg: Imperial Academy of Sciences, 1912), 27.

25   *Relationship of India and China*, ninth-century Arabic text translated and published in London in 1733. See Abu Zayd Hasan et al., *Ancient Accounts of India and China by Two Mohammedan Travellers* (1733), 5. European

fascination not only with the Orient but also with mediaeval Arab travel radiates from this 1733 frontispiece. Borges believed that publication of *The Arabian Nights* in Europe a few years earlier gave rise to the Romantic movement.

26   *Kevatta Sutta*, quoted in *Chu-fan-chi*, 28.

27   Jataka 543, from *The Jataka, or Stories of the Buddha's Former Births*, trans. E. B. Cowell and W. H. D. Rouse, vol. VI (Cambridge, 1907), 93.

28   Ibid.

29   See Rudolf Wittkower, *Allegory and the Migration of Symbols* (1938), 77. Wittkower cites the identification of Rukh and Garuda made by Kalipadra Mitra in 'The bird and serpent myth', *Quarterly Journal of the Mythic Society* 16 (1926): 189.

30   R. Paul Scofield and Ken W. S. Ashwell, 'Rapid somatic expansion causes the brain to lag behind: The case of the brain and behaviour of New Zealand's Haast's eagle', *Journal of Vertebrate Paleontology* 29, no. 3 (2009). Italics are my emphasis.

31   There are several versions of the lament for Korotangi. This one was collected in Rotorua by Governor George Grey and published in 1853. It is also the one which Barry Mitcalfe chose in the 1960s for his translation, used here. He had the advantage over other translators of being a fine poet in his own right.

32   Julius von Haast, *Transactions of the Royal Society of New Zealand* vol. 14 (1881), 104 (see also vol. 22, 1889, 500).

33   Walter Buller, *Manual of the Birds of New Zealand* (1882), 67.

34   Henry, *Ancient Tahiti*, 123.

35   Ibid., 126.

36   John Williams, *A Narrative of Missionary Enterprises in the South Sea Islands* (London, 1840), 56.

37   M. P. K. Sorrenson (ed.), *Na To Hoa Aroha, From Your Dear Friend: The Correspondence of Sir Apirana Ngata and Sir Peter Buck, 1925–50*, 3 vols (Auckland: Auckland University Press, 1986–88).

38   Marco Polo, *The Description of the World*, A. C. Moule and Paul Pelliot edn (London, 1938). The rest of the Marco Polo quotations in this chapter are from the same source.

39   *Chu-fan-chi*, 153. This 'wonderful land' possibly refers to Yemen. Even in the 1970s, the great travel writer Norman Lewis reported, Yemenis dreaded the light of the setting sun, would not look at it, covered their heads during the event, and that west-facing windows in their houses were fitted with translucent but opaque material.

40   Ibn Battuta, *The Rihla, or A Gift to Those Who Contemplate the Wonders of Cities and the Marvels of Travelling* (1355).

41   Chau Ju-kua, *His Work . . . Entitled Chu-fan-chi*, trans. Friedrich Hirth and W. W. Rockhill (1911), 134.

42   Ibid., 172.

43   Ibid., 31.

44   Master Zhuang, *The Zhuangzi*, trans. A. C., Graham (1981). See also *Heaven and Earth: 120 Album Leaves from a Ming Encyclopedia: San-ts'ai t'u-hui* [1610] (London: John Goodall, 1979).

45   On the voyage of the Tainui canoe from Raiatea to New Zealand, it is recounted that the vessel was nearly overwhelmed by 80 sea monsters which crowded around the vessel. The navigator, Riu-ki-uta, who had summoned them as guides, had to lie down in the bow and call out: *Don't come aboard, fall away, You are female, I am male, You come by the lower path, I by the upper.* This clearly echoes the contrasts of yin-yang, although the ancestors of Māori left east Asia at least 5000 years ago.

46   William Frederick Mayers, *A Chinese Reader's Manual* (Mayers, 1874), part I.

47   Paul W. Kroll, *Studies in Medieval Taoism and the Poetry of Li Po* (New York: Routledge, 2009).

48   The Korotangi is no longer on display in Wellington. It was taken back and presented to Waikato-Tainui during a ceremony to mark the Deed of Settlement between the Crown and iwi, which included an apology for the land confiscations after the New Zealand Wars. The carving is still occasionally seen in public, amidst the regalia of the Māori king.

49   James Watt et al., *The World of Khubilai Khan: Chinese Art in the Yuan Dynasty* (New York: MetPublications, 2010).

50   'The discovery of New Zealand by Kupe as related by Te Matorohanga', *Journal of the Polynesian Society* 22, no. 87 (1913): 125.

51   These four excerpts are from, respectively: White, *The Ancient History of the Maori*, vol. 2, p. 188; ibid., vol. 7, p. 80; ibid., vol. 3, chapter 6; Barry Brailsford, *Song of Waitaha* (Christchurch, 1994).

52   The book in question, *Song of Waitaha*, has attracted fierce criticism for its poeticised prose, lack of stated sources and some of its wilder claims of extreme antiquity for the Waitaha settlement. But it is derived from the writings of Taare Te Maiharoa, one of the most trusted South Island Māori historians, who gives the same information about the probable landfall, near Kaikōura, of the *Uruao* canoe on which the Waitaha sailed. See *Journal of the Polynesian Society* 27, no. 107 (1918): 137–51.

About the author

Peter Walker grew up in Christchurch and began his writing career as a journalist in Wellington and then Sydney. He moved to London in 1986 and joined *The Independent* and later the *Independent on Sunday* where he was Foreign Editor. He also wrote for the *Literary Review*, the *Financial Times* books pages and *Granta*. He is the author of the historical memoir *The Fox Boy* (Bloomsbury, 2001), set in Taranaki, and his first novel *The Courier's Tale* (Bloomsbury, 2010), set in Italy and the court of Henry VIII. In 2011 he was a Randell Cottage fellow in Wellington and began another novel, *Some Here Among Us* (Bloomsbury, 2015). He now lives on an orange orchard near Ninety Mile Beach in the Far North.

Acknowledgements

I was lucky to find several experts — palaeozoologists, ornithologists, geneticists — who, overcoming their wonder at my ignorance, helped very generously with the scientific chapter of the story that opened in 1872 in a swamp. The following list is not complete, but I am especially indebted to Sandy Bartle, Trevor Worthy, Mike Bunce, Peter Wills, Paul Scofield and Phil Millener, and of course to Phil Wood, who led most of us to the caves in the first place.

I needed a good deal of assistance with the Māori and Polynesian material. There is a protocol now in place in New Zealand to consult with iwi on matters concerning their history and mythology. This is not only a question of courtesy — it is of huge benefit to the writer as well. But it is not always easy to find someone with the inclination to assist. So I am particularly grateful to Buddy Mikaere, Pita Turei, Ross Calman, the great sculptor Brett Graham, Sir Tipene O'Regan (who first suggested that I write about the Ngāi Tahu claim) and Ken McAnertney (who drove me to several sites of ancient rock art, and through whose eyes I could half-see the South Island still as Waitaha territory). I also must mention those who helped with translations from Māori, including Anthony Hoete, Aubrey Hoete, Te Raukura Solomon and Kathy Walker, and also those who know the Māori world (and the art world) better than I do and showed me where to turn for help — Jenny Todd, Neil Pardington, Monty Soutar, Loni Hutchison, Whina Te Whiu, Maia Nuku, Sue Smith and Kriselle Baker.

Above all I am grateful to Albert Refiti, who from the start was extremely generous with advice, source material, dictionaries and his wide knowledge of the space-time — the vā he might call it — of culture across the Pacific.

The book was begun more than ten years ago but for a few years before that I had the help of early listeners — people who were good enough to sit around and discuss a subject they'd never heard of before. Was it worth a book? Where would it lead? There were probably many more but I have clear memories of sitting up late in north London with Jan Dalley and Sid Motion, on a hillside at dusk in France with Brian and Ruth Cathcart, and in a house on New Year's Eve in the snowy woods of Connecticut with Dan and Sam Witters. Sue Hancock was always generous in her appraisals of the project, as was Elizabeth Woabank who read a very early draft — too early really, to be out and about — and saw its flaws but also saw potential.

Other, later readers of the book or parts of it — Pita Turei, Jenny Todd, Sarah Herriot, John McIntyre, Alison Copland, Alex Frame, Barry Fraser, David Godwin, Jim Clad — gave me encouragement which was needed at the time, as rejection slips had started to arrive. Then there were the great friends, mostly in the South Island, who came on the road or marched into the Southern Alps with me in search of Harpagornis, or who put me up for a few nights in sight of the Alps — Peter and Annabel Graham at Camla, my cousins, John and Nan Fogarty, at Bridle Path Road, and my old friend 'Paddy McMahon' who wanted to be in the book but also didn't want to be in it and is therefore hidden behind a nom de guerre.

I have special thanks as well to all the following: Fiona Elworthy, who led us to a cave on her farm in Canterbury with a very clear pictograph of the eagle on the ceiling, made by a stone-age artist who possibly risked life to go there and make it; Mark Adams who has been a real friend of the book and taken some terrific photographs for its pages; Penry Buckley who led me through the quadrangles of Oxford, and later set out on great library and internet searches for me; Jacqui Mitcalfe who allowed the use of her late husband's beautiful translation of the song to Korotangi; Trevor Worthy, who allowed me to quote freely from his own writing, and Jeremy Evison who allowed me to quote from his father's ground-breaking works, Te Waipounamu and The Long Dispute, which not only outlined South Island inter-racial history but were so powerful and lucid that they helped change it.

Encouragement and assistance of different kinds from Sarah Duckworth, Bobby Newson, Vargie and Pam Johnson, Austin Trevett, Penny Bieder, Joelle Smaniotto, Tim Gorton, Dame Anne Salmond, staff at Canterbury Museum, Richard McArley, Sophie Torney and Tristram and Diane Clayton were greatly appreciated, along with the warm support, insight and fine judgement of Nicola Legat and her editorial and design team, Rachel Scott, Anna Bowbyes and Sarah Elworthy.

MASSEY
UNIVERSITY
PRESS

First published in 2024 by Massey University Press
Private Bag 102904, North Shore Mail Centre
Auckland 0745, New Zealand
www.masseypress.ac.nz

Design by Sarah Elworthy
Cover artwork adapted with permission from a woodcut
by Noa Noa von Bassewitz

The moral right of the author has been asserted

A catalogue record for this book is available from the
National Library of New Zealand

Printed and bound in Singapore by Markono Print Media Pte Ltd

ISBN: 978-1-99-101671-3
eISBN: 978-1-99-101681-2

The assistance of Creative New Zealand is gratefully acknowledged
by the publisher